Heavenly Realm Publishing
Houston, Texas

ISBN—13- 978-1-93791154-6

Library of Congress Control Number: 2013911402
Church Hurt: How to Heal & Overcome It/ Stephanie Franklin

This book is printed on acid free paper.

Printed in the United States of America

All scripture notations, unless otherwise indicated, are taken from The Holy Bible-King James version.2007.

Published By:
Heavenly Realm Publishing
PO Box 682532
Houston, Texas 77268
Toll Free: 1-866-216-0696
Fax: 281-520-4059

CHURCH HURT

"How to Heal & Overcome It"

STEPHANIE FRANKLIN

TABLE OF CONTENTS

CHURCH HURT
"How to Heal & Overcome It"

BOOKS BY STEPHANIE

FICTION NOVELS & MOTIVATIONAL BOOKS:

1. When Ramona Got Her Groove Back from God
2. My Song of Solomon
3. My Song of Solomon *Prayer Journal*
4. God Loves Thugs Too!
5. *The Locker Room Experience: For the Struggling Athlete & Coach, & Tips on How to Get Recruited in Sports*

MINISTRY BOOKS & WORKBOOK:

6. Position Your Faith for Great Success
7. Position Your Faith for Great Success *Workbook*
8. The Purpose Chaser: *For Children Ages 5 to 12*
9. Church Hurt: *How to Heal & Overcome It*

CHURCH HURT

How to Heal & Overcome It.

I dedicate this to You Heavenly Father.
Thank you for restoring me.

Also for every person who has been hurt in
the church. I understand. My prayer is that you
allow Christ to be your restorer…

ACKNOWLEDGEMENTS

To all of my family and friends who play such a vital role in my life, purpose, and ministry. You all know who you are and how special you are to me. May God bless you with the greater and may He continue to bless you, your families, and your prosperity. Thank you all always.

A special thanks to my momma. Thank you for supporting me through all of my persecutions, upsets, setbacks, dilemmas, triumphs, and disappointments. I love you so much, and for being the best momma in the whole world.

To Kay, you are the best. Thank you for your countless prayers and support. We have been through so much and yet we've made it. God has seen us through it all. He is so faithful and He is worthy of all the praise.

PREFACE

I know you're thinking that the church is the best place in the world—
and it's the safest place in the world, but that is not always true. I am not
bashing the church; I am simply being honest about what happens in the
church. It seems nobody wants to either admit it, or they're too scared to
tell anybody for fear that nobody will believe them, or that they will be
judged or even kicked out of the church. Maybe the fact is that their hurt
is so deep that they cannot even talk about it, or get it out to release it
because it is too deep to expose or uproot. This is the type of "church
hurt" that I am going to be discussing in this book. God has given me a
cry and a deep concern for the church, and for those who have gone
through this, or may still be going through this at this present time. I am
a living witness that if you are a victim of this, you can be set free, healed,
and can overcome every part of it to get your life back. Whatever you do,
DO NOT GIVE UP! Please know as you read this book, it is not a book to
bash the church or to make every person who attends church an evil
person; or that they are hell bound. It is not that type of book. I do not
have a hell to put anybody, and I do not choose to anyway. I am merely
sharing that if you are a victim of church hurt, you can be healed and
can overcome it and have true victory in Jesus Christ.

I am reminded of Nehemiah in the bible *(Book of Nehemiah)*.
Nehemiah was being attacked by so-called church folks. Some would call
them haters. They saw the call and purpose on Nehemiah's life, which
made him an easy target. Does this fit you? The attackers were not lay
members; they were those in high rank and authority *(Pastors, associate
pastors, preacher's, bishops, deacons, head of finance leader, etc.)*. They
did not want to see Nehemiah promoted and doing the will of God. So
they tried to stop him any way they could. Does this fit you again?

Christians must be in a place in their Christian walk not to place high leaders in such high standard that they place them over God. Any person whether a Christian believer or an unbeliever, saved or lost, in a high ranking position is not exempt from having the potential of sinning, falling, making a mistake, or being used by the devil. The devil is shrewd in his evil intentions; he will use anybody he can in order to stop the will of God in the church and out of the church; and in the lives of God's people. In fact, he attempts to use more Christian believers and faithful church goers than unbelievers and non-church goers. Therefore, if you are a believer you should constantly pray for those in high ranking clergy, church goers, and church lay members on your daily prayer list each day. The devil strives to attack their minds, thoughts, and actions in such a way that deceives them to think they're right while operating in the mist of their attacks. This proves to be a Spirit of Error [1 John 4:6]. The Spirit of Error, a stronghold, works best when there is an ignorance of God's Word. Believers who do not read and study the Word of God for themselves are driven to believe false actions and information that appears to be the truth. This type of spirit works best with a lying spirit, perverse (lust) spirit, pride spirit, control spirit, and divination spirit. There are many leaders who operate in these types of areas while some may not realize it. There are Christians who are active in the church across the globe who are challenged and attacked by this spirit from leaders each week. The devil loves to use those who are in high rank because if he can stop them and use them to bring confusion, nobody will come to church, believe God's Word, and the Will of God for His people and church will be shattered. It does the devil no good to attack his own because they already belong to him. He wants to pull God's church, it's divine purpose, and God's people from God's true plan, unity, and love for one another—which is God's Will. We as Christians, church goers must take a stand and make a conscious decision to be committed to the

Lord, to the church, and to all church members in such a way that we love, show respect, and are always on guard not to allow the enemy to use us against one another. It is time to win back God's church.

Below I am going to give you three commitments. I challenge you to commit your life back to God and to the church. Read below on how to do it.

THE THREE COMMITMENTS:

I encourage you to make three commitments on a daily basis before leaving your house and before entering the church.

1. <u>**Recognize the level of excellence you are called to each day**</u> in the ministry and in various Christian groups, small groups, organizations, functions, fellowships, and relationships and strive to live up to it or them.

2. <u>**Rely on God to be committed and stay committed.**</u> Rely and realize that this is a battle that you cannot win alone or by your own power, strength, and abilities. It takes everybody as a community of believers to work together in unity to fulfill the Will of God for your life and for the operation, function and order of the church.

3. <u>**Reach after those who need help.**</u> It is important to remember that there are hurting people outside of the church as well as in the church, and it is <u>not</u> about piety emotions and feelings, it is about being in position to be used by God, in an humble state to receive from God, and excited about the change in not only your life, but in the lives of others.

There is not a picture perfect Christian. So you must remember that if you do not want to be considered, and expected to be a picture perfect Christian, pastor, ministry leader, staff, church worker, ministry volunteer, church member, please **do not expect** others to be a picture perfect Christian, pastor, ministry leader, staff, church worker, ministry volunteer, church member because you will not find one; and you will always be disappointed and in a place of the critical eye or looking to pass judgment on others. Make a conscious decision to strive and be committed to live and follow the Three Commitments each day of your life.

THE MALFUNCTION OF THE CHURCH

The church has malfunctioned and has gone away from the true call of the function of the church. It has formatted itself to fit the people's selfish desires rather than the desire and the call that Jesus has placed on the church. He never ordained the church to function from a flesh state, but from a Spirit state. Because of this, it has formulated what I will call a click spirit—organizational groupings, rather than the leading and the grouping of the Holy Spirit; only for the edification of the Lord.

These clicks and groupings have brought so many unbiblical truths that have no substance to stand on and are based on human ideas, control over the church, the clergy, the administration, and over the entire body of Christ. These <u>schisms</u>—split divisions, beliefs, confusions, out of control actions, attitudes, and activities have literally divided churches to a degree that they have closed and have never re-opened again.

Unethical opinions have discouraged and/or even turned away many Saints of God from the church; and some even to unbelief. As a result, many Christians have left the church because of this reason. These unbiblical, unprincipled actions should not be so. The church should be a place of restoration, reconciliation, and a unified gathering place of praise and worship to the Father. It should also be a place of healing, salvation, a safe-haven, temple of faith, love, and a Spirit fed and <u>biblical</u> taught body of Christ. These are the things that were important for Jesus as He taught the disciples while He lived on earth, and to fulfill the prophesy. In 1 Corinthians 1:2, it states that through the church of God, we should be Saints of God, called Saints of God—which is called of Jesus Christ. This must be instilled in the hearts of believers in God all across the world as we follow the principles of God and for the church.

God is calling back His church. He is calling back His people. He is calling back the backsliders. He is calling back the hurting and the wounded. He is calling back those who have left the church and have made their home their church. God is raising up real pastors and removing disobedient, unclean pastors that have operated in the pastoral position either because of generational calling—the mom or dad was the senior pastors and they past the mantel down to the child without hearing from God first. By this decision, it has ruined and has contaminated the church. From this blinded, unbiblical and selfish choice, it has brought the Spirit of Pride among other evil spirits in the church. It formulated the attitude of:

- "This is my dad's or mom's church and they have chosen me to pastor/lead in this position so you better listen to me",

- or, "Ya'll better listen to me or I'm ganna' remove you out of your position if you don't let me have my way",

- or, "I'm all that because my dad/mom is all that",

- or, "I can sin in the church because my parents are pastors and they pretty much let me do whatever I want to do",

- or, "I'm the pastor, you do what I tell you to do. I don't care if God told you that or not, I'm the one you listen to",

- or, "We can build so many churches, and we can have so much money, all we gotta' do is run this church just like a for-profit business; and make the church give and use that money to build more churches, and we will never go wrong",

- or, "Just sleep with me, my wife or husband will never find out. I can make you happy. I have a lot of money and I can take care of you (and if you have children, them too)",

- or, "I'm a minister, elder, evangelist, deacon, deaconess, reverend, musician, teacher, or preacher and nobody's gon' take my place",

- or, "If she or he put their mouth on me one more time, I'm gon' beat her or him down",

- or, "I'm gon' stay faithful so I can take the pastor's place one day",

- or, "She or he was just a sinner that just got saved, how she or he gon' come in this church and become a preacher over night?"

- or, "How she or he gon' sing secular music one day, and the next get saved and sing gospel music and call themselves saved?"

- or, "She or he don't even go to church, how they gon' be saved?"

- And the list goes on…

There are many more quotes and examples that I can give but I do not have enough room in this book to fit them all. This type of proud talk and arrogant activity has torn the church apart and has brought so many schisms within the church; when it was never God's Will in the first place. No one has a position to judge anyone [Matthew 7:1]. God is the only judge.

Just about every person I either have spoken to or have run across have the same attitude and a story to tell of how they have been hurt in the church in some sort of way. Of course I am not speaking of every church and certainly not every pastor or leader, but hurt is prevalent all over the world in so many that cannot be counted. I used to judge without trying to understand why this is so, and the Lord comforted and ministered to me and allowed me to know that it is not the pastors, leaders, or the people in the church that have brought so much confusion and division, it is the devil. The bible says that the devil comes to steal, kill, and to <u>destroy</u> [John 10:10]. It was and still is the devil's plan to destroy the plan, praise, worship, anointing, the anointed, the love, unity, gifts, the call, and the glory of the Lord in the church. But God assures us through His Word that He will get the glory. He is still God in the church, and He will prove that He brings life, and that His people will have it more abundantly [John 10:10]. God is not through with His people yet. He is still able to save, heal, and restore anybody. So if you have gone or are going through this hurt, anger, disappointment, and/or confusion, I encourage you to allow God to minister comfort and healing to you; to understand that you should not be mad at those who have hurt or disappointed you in the church. You should be mad at the devil and begin to pray against the forces of darkness [Ephesians 6:10-18], and ask God to cancel every evil demonic assignment and plan to cancel God's temple [church], people, glory, plan and promise in Jesus name.

Many pastors and leaders have been placed in major roles in the church based on their ability to speak well, or by familiar association, or hidden agendas; and they lack the real depth of the Holy Spirit and the heart of Jesus Christ. There have also been many pastors and leaders that have ordained, placed, and elected other pastors, leaders, elders, preachers, reverends, youth leaders, youth pastors, women pastors, missionaries, evangelists, etc. to positions that they did not have experience or lack the love for the people to fulfill the work of that particular position. What happens is, they end up or ended up wounding the Saints of God, lay members, babes in Christ [those that just got saved—accepted Christ into their life] and as a result, they have hurt and have discouraged them out of the church in packs. Many people are struggling before they step foot in the church and to have things of this sort to happen to them is very detrimental. Some never recover or come back. But God is faithful and He is calling those back. God is the One who calls all of us. No one has the right to call or to choose who they want in a position in the church. God calls and chooses through the direction of the Holy Spirit as the pastor/leader hears from God. Pastors/leaders who chooses without praying and seeking the Heart of God is operating in a Spirit of control—wanting all of the power; which is not God's Power. God will never give anyone, whether in the flesh or in the Spirit the ability, control or the pleasure to think or feel that they have all the power to make decisions or to change situations. **NOT SO**. God is the **only** One who controls and should be the **only** One who makes all of the decisions for the church. God is not a Man that He should lie, neither the son of man that He should repent [Numbers 23:19-20]. He never has to go back and clean up His mess because He has no mess to clean up. He never has to go back and heal someone that He has wounded because He does not come to wound us. He is the God of love [1 John 4:8] and compassion—even for those who have sinned and have fallen short of His glory [Romans 3:23]. He is still merciful to forgive through repentance and will sow grace to those who stand in need of it [Romans 10:9-13]. But we as Saints of God, people of God, believers in Christ, Christians in faith have to constantly be aware of how we treat people in the church, in our communities, on our jobs, in our daily activities, and all around us. I realize that no one is perfect, but we should strive for perfection on a daily basis—perfecting those areas of struggle constantly.

If you are not mad at me by now or have not decided to throw this book away, I would like to talk about the chapters of the book next. I hope you will receive what you need in-so-that this book will change your life forever. I pray it will heal, love, embrace, bring understanding, forgiveness, restoration, recovery, and/or bring unity in your life and in others, you know.

Because you have gotten to this point in the book, either you kept reading because you can identify with this book because you are a victim of church hurt, or you know somebody in the church who have been hurt in the church. I hope you get what you need either way and that it will bless your life in a changeable way. Here we go…

QUENCH NOT THE HOLY SPIRIT:
You must be careful not to quench the Holy Spirit [1 Thessalonians 5:19]. Many churches, pastors, and leaders *(Ministers, reverends, deacons, missionaries, evangelists, and so forth)* quench the Holy Spirit every time the church doors open.

An example I will give as I speak of quenching the Holy Spirit is this. There was a time I was visiting a church and as the praise and worship went forth, the Holy Spirit and the anointing feel in the place and healing and breakthroughs begin to happen. As they began to change the atmosphere, the pastor comes up to the podium and silenced the congregation with a slow, quiet, speech that had nothing to do with what the Holy Spirit was doing at that moment. He immediately quenched the Holy Spirit (drained, stopped, hindered) the presence of the Lord. People were shouting and crying, many were up with their hands up, others were running around in the Spirit, and the pastor told them to stop as if he was in control. It must be understood that we as leaders, God's children, Christians, and believers are not in control. The Holy Spirit controls, directs, and leads the church atmosphere and congregation because He knows what we need at that point in time. When leaders do what they want to do, they miss the Will of God for God's people, which are to save, heal, and deliver. **It is the Will of the Father that we all BELIEVE.** If you are a pastor or leader who has been operating in this type of way, you should take heed and begin to listen and obey the Holy Spirit right away. Many times pastors and leaders are operating in error and do not even know it. You must constantly be sensitive to the Holy Spirit as it directs. Many churches have lost their congregations because of this— people leaving because the pastor will not obey and allow the Holy Spirit to lead and heal God's people. If the church that God has chosen you to lead has gone down in membership, check how you are operating. Check if you are obeying the Holy Spirit. This is one of the main malfunctions in the church—disobedience.

LACK OF LEADERSHIP:

Because of lack of leadership in the church, it has opened the door to the devil to attack the church as a whole, the government *(taking prayer out of school)*, schools *(fighting, bullying, drugs, gangs, suicide)*, various ministries in the church, associations, businesses, God's people, and their purpose. But it is time for the church, pastor's, leaders in ministry, and God's people to come together as a community of believers and win back the church, God's people, our government, unethical pastor's, the schools *(putting prayer back in the schools)*, and come together with a corporate chain of prayer. In Matthew 18:19 it states that where two or more touching and agreeing on the same thing, God promises to be in the mist of every situation or problem. We must come together and allow God's purpose and promise to operate through each of us as a unified whole. As we obey, signs and wonders will occur on the earth like never before, miracles will begin to happen right before our eyes, and God will be glorified.

The Initial Attack [Part 1]

◊　　　◊　　　◊　　　◊　　　◊　　　◊　　　◊

IT IS A NORMAL SUNDAY MORNING service and your thoughts are totally on the Lord until someone comes up to you and ask why you didn't speak to them when you came in the church. Your first initial thought is, *"why in the world are they coming up to me with this drama during morning service?"* Try this one, before you can take your seat, someone in the ministry comes up to you as if they were casing you out and attacks you and says their false case, *"Why didn't you sign up to work on the clean-up committee*

> *Do not listen and allow people to rule over you and your life. Do not allow people to have control over your mind, do not allow people to have power over your life and past. If you have repented, God have forgiven you for what you have done the second you asked Him to.*

after the musical on last week? You act like you too good to clean up?" Or, you may even have encountered the *"married"* Pastor calling you in his office and saying, *"I've been watching you for a very long time now and I have noticed how beautiful you are, and I want to know can I show you how much I can make you feel good. Will you sleep with me? I promise I won't tell nobody, and I promise I'll fill your bank account up just right."* Or lastly, let's try this one, *"I know you're the pastor of this church, I just wanna' tell you that you are so fine. I can't keep my eyes off of you so I decided to approach you first. I know you are married but I don't care, I can please you better than she or he can."*

When these things happen or are said to you, it throws you off and your first thought is a state of shock, anger, resentment, fear, hatred, you want to leave the church, curse them out, and/or give them a peace of your mind. You may even go as far as to knocking them out right in the middle of the church service; which is supposed to be a peaceful place for worship and praising the Lord. In the Pastor's position, your first initial thought is to go run to the police and put him or her in jail, or sue him or her for every penny they and the church has.

If you have encountered these attacks, you should never shun away from the church. You should draw closer to the Lord. In these types of situations it is very important to be close to the Lord. Without this relationship, many detrimental things can happen. Being close to the Lord and listening to His voice will never allow you to do something crazy or out of control. God will always lead you to do and say Godly things. He will never lead you astray. You can lead you astray, but God will never lead you astray.

Another type of attack you may have is people.

You may have the attack of people judging a sin you committed while in the church. You may be dealing with people in the church judging, watching, lying on you, and constantly reminding you of the sin you committed before. I want to encourage you. As I stated before, God is the only One who has the right to judge you. Yes, you messed up, and yes you did commit a sin that was wrong, but that gives no human on this earth the right or the power to judge you. **Do not listen** and allow people to rule over you and your life. Do not allow people to have control over your mind, do not allow people to have power over your life and past. If you repented, God has forgiven you for what you have done the second you asked Him to. The same people who are judging and constantly reminding you about your past are the ones you need to pray for. They need to be healed, forgiven, and need to allow God to remove the log [beam] that is in their eyes against you [Luke 6:41-42].

> *For with what judgment ye judge, ye shall be judged: and with what measure ye mete, it shall be measured to* you again.
> **Matthew 7:2**

I have learned that people take pleasure in teasing, picking and judging a person who comes off loving, or appear to be weak. When they see that they can hurt you, they will continue to do so until you take charge and refuse not to allow them [the devil] to, nor have power over you, your mind, your past, your day, or your life. I am reminded of this passage of scripture in [John 4:7-28] concerning Jesus and the adulteress woman at the well. One of the most profound things I found in this passage of scripture was that He did not condemn her of her sin. No one has the right to judge anyone because we all have sinned and have fallen short of God's glory. There are no special sins nor are there little sins or big sins. God is no respect of persons, He see all sin the same [Romans 2:11]. So, just as the ones who are laughing, picking or talking bad about you and your past, they too are dealing with their sins and struggles that are not pleasing to God. You are not alone. God is with you and He will fight for you but you cannot allow people to keep you in a tormented dark shell of your past that God has forgiven and delivered you out of. Be healed today. Make this the day you say to yourself that you are no longer going to allow people to dictate, control or have power over you, your life, your past, your calling, your love, your mind, or your future.

Speak over your life by repeating these words of faith daily until you feel freedom within yourself and see manifestations in your life:

> *"I thank you Lord that You have granted me the power to no longer allow people to dictate, control or have power over my life, my past, my calling, my love, my mind, or my future. In Jesus Name, Amen."*

FOR YOUR NOTES:

Going Through the Fire

◊   ◊   ◊   ◊   ◊   ◊   ◊

9 F DANIEL, HANANIAH, MISHAEL, AZARIAH, better known as Shadrach, Meshach, and Abednego knew they were going to GO THROUGH THE FIRE, they wouldn't have ever went to the King's palace in the first place. If they knew that they were going to be persecuted—Daniel would have never interpreted the King's dream. If he knew they were going to GO THROUGH THE FIRE, they would have said forget it we'll rather play sports like most youthful boys. But no, Daniel was on a mission for the Lord just as

> *The Word of God teaches His people how to fight the devil. Again, you cannot fight the devil with your own power and strength. You will lose every time. You fight the devil with the Word of God (the bible).*

Shadrach, Meshach, and Abednego were. They were well disciplined. They all fasted ten days eating only vegetables while all of the other youths ate whatever they wanted [with no discipline] [Daniel 2:8-15]. I believe this is how the fire never consumed them.

Daniel was a leader and he knew the purpose that God had for him which is why he did not play around like all of the other youths. He fasted because he knew that God would honor his sacrifice and move on his behalf. His first fire came because, well as we all know, from haters. Daniel, Shadrach, Meshach, and Abed-nego were highly favored by the King Nebuchadnezzar. He felt that there were none like them and that they were knowledgeable in learning and wise. Kind of like when a Pastor see something special in one of his members as a result of the anointing on their life, and as a result, somebody in the church always have to get jealous. It happened right after Daniel interpreted the dream and got promoted by the King—He made him ruler over the whole province of Babylon, and chief of the governors over all the wise men of Babylon [Daniel 2:48-49]. And that is when the church folks started to watch them like a hawk and tell on them like they're lives were so perfect. The sad thing about it was that Daniel, Shadrach, Meshach, and Abed-nego were not doing anything wrong. They did not serve nor bow down and worship other god's, and because of hatred and jealousy, Shadrach, Meshach, and Abed-nego were thrown in the FIRE. That was their test. I'm sure that you have experienced this before; or you may be experiencing this right now. It's not an easy thing to go through especially when you are totally innocent. I want to encourage you today to be encouraged, because if God came through for Shadrach, Meshach, and Abed-nego in the fiery furnace—not allowing them to get burned up, I know He can come through for you. Wow, that is some faith isn't it? It takes faith to trust God totally when the enemy is before you and bringing false accusations against you. But I have never seen the righteous forsaken, nor his seed beg bread [Psalm 37:25]. Then God says in His word that He's not a Man that He would lie, nor the son of man that He should repent.... If God promise you that he was going to do something for you, you better believe that He will keep His word. Not only because He wants to, but because He has to [Numbers 23:19-20]. Greater is He that is within you, than he that is in the world [1 John 4:4]. Greater is God that is within you when you want to strike back and give them a piece of your mind or go ballistic on them. God's precious love is what stops you and allows you to understand that it is not them but satan operating in them. See, satan does not want you to make it. He does not want you to succeed. He does not want your life to prosper. He does not want your ministry to be promoted. He does not want your anointing to operate because then you will help too many people and they will be saved, healed, and delivered. He hates that so he tries to come against you by using weak people to do it. In Ephesians 6:12, it says that *"we do not wrestle (fight, argue, pick, hate, gossip, backbite, snitch, complain) against flesh and blood (people, church folk, unbelievers), but we wrestle (fight, argue, pick, hate, gossip, backbite, snitch, complain) against principalities, against the rulers of the darkness of this world, against spiritual wickedness in high places"*. You should be encouraged and know that God is with you and He is fighting for you. You should take your scriptures on faith, promise and protection and speak them out loud as you speak them over your life on a daily basis. God will never allow his people to be moved nor will He allow the enemy to defeat you. He will always come through for you. He may not come when you want Him to, but He will be right on time. The Word of God teaches His people how to fight the devil. Again, you cannot fight the devil with your own power and strength. You will lose every time. You fight the devil with the Word of God (the bible). Speak the Word over your life. You must speak the Word by faith believing that God will move and the devil must flee. Let me give you a couple of examples: Shadrach, Meshach, and Abed-nego did not ever get into a fighting match with the Jews who ran their mouth against them. They simply let King Nebuchadnezzar know that the God they serve is able to deliver them from the burning fiery furnace and He will deliver them out of the hand of the king [Daniel 3:12-30]. Upon hearing this, the devil used the king and tried to make matters worse by commanding the furnace to be heated seven more times than it was originally supposed to be [verse 19]. It does not matter how evil the devil uses his people to come against you, if God promised you that He will deliver and protect you, you better believe He will keep His Word. And He did just that in verse 25-27, the fire never burned Shadrach, Meshach, and Abed-nego. I will go so far to show you that when you have faith and turn every person or situation that is against you over to the Lord, He will be right there in the mist of trouble to help and to deliver you just as He was with those four in the fiery furnace [Daniel 3:25]. I have something else awesome, in verse 27 it says that **THE FIRE HAD NO POWER**, nor was a hair on their head

> *Going through the fire may hurt, but it is good because it gives God the opportunity to prove Who He is.*

singed, neither were their coats changed, nor did the smell of the **FIRE STENCH THEIR CLOTHES**. I want to encourage you that God is faithful to perform anything that He has promised you. He is a God of His Word. Greater is He that is within you than He that is in the world [1 John 4:4]. God made their enemies admit how powerful God was in verse 27. God will make your enemies have to speak highly of you to others. He will make your enemies bless you. God is just this faithful in your life through any hurt, anger, or attacks that have made you a prey. Going through the fire may hurt, but it is good because it gives God the opportunity to prove Who He is. God is good at making the devil out of a liar [John 8:44]. I'm not saying that you should look forward to going through the fire, but when or if that time comes, and you are trusting in the Lord already, just know that it is only a test and that it will not burn or consume you. It will only make you stronger in faith to know that God will prevail in your storm, your struggle, or your attack whether it is happening in the church, on your job, or in your personal life. Do you believe that? Good, I thought you'd agree. Praise God! Go forward in the strength of the Lord and know who you are and do not allow satan to think he has power over you. You have power over him and all of his evil doers through Christ Jesus, Who was sent to help, guide, protect, love, and defeat satan each time he tries to come against you each day.

The Initial Attack [Part 2]

◊　　　◊　　　◊　　　◊　　　◊　　　◊　　　◊

HAT WOULD YOU DO IF YOU were in the Lion's Den with roaring lions that were on their way over to devour you [Daniel 6]? Would you run and hide? Would you try to fight them like you were going to win? Or would you pray like Daniel did? Well, I have learned the higher you get in God, the higher the attacks will come. This attack for Daniel came after another promotion. The King just promoted Daniel to be over the entire kingdom, as a result of him finding an excellent spirit in him—which was the Spirit of the living God

> *Neither one of us have a Heaven or hell to put anybody. We are all working to better ourselves on daily basis. This is why it is important to watch our actions whether active in the church, or active in the community.*

deep down on the inside of him. Right after that, here come the haters—hatin' church folks again. Right when you get promoted, the devil will use people to stop your promotion, which is your purpose. But what the haters do not realize is that they're not coming against you, they are coming against God. They do not realize you were sent to do a work for the Lord. It is unfortunate that they are looking at the flesh and not at the Spirit—to know that God is going to bless them through you if they just praise God for your promotion. If they get with you as you do the will of God, they will be blessed. The devil has literally blinded their eyes not to see. I want you to understand that they cannot stop you, but only stop themselves. The bible declares in Daniel chapter 6 verse 4 that: "…the presidents and princes sought to find occasion against Daniel concerning the Kingdom; **but they could find none occasion nor fault**; forasmuch as he was faithful, neither was there any error or fault found in him." As you look in that passage of scripture, you will see that they could not find any fault in him, only that he was faithful. People will try to find fault in anything they can to make you look wrong, but it will not work because God will protect and He will fight for you just as He did for Daniel.

They had the nerve to throw Daniel in a den of lions [Daniel 6:17]. Now, Daniel has these ferocious lions staring him right in the face ready to eat him alive. But Daniel prayed and believed the God we all serve, and God kept His Word, He came through once again for Daniel. Not only because He loved him, but because God made a promise to him. The bible states in verse 22 of that same chapter that God sent his angel and shut the lions' mouths so that the loins did not hurt him because he was innocent. Now can you say the same thing? If they threw you in a den of lions would the angel be able to save you? Or would the lions devour you because you're one of the haters? Are you one of the church folk's causing trouble and bringing lies against God's people? We as Christians have to be careful how we come against God's people and put our mouths on them like they are not anointed of God, especially when they have not done anything wrong. The bible says not to touch God's anointed, nor do His prophet's no harm [1 Chronicles 16:22, Psalms 105:15]. Neither one of us have a Heaven or hell to put anybody. We are all working to better ourselves on a daily basis. This is why it is important to watch our actions whether active in the church, or active in the community. Pastors and leaders are not exempt from this type of behavior. In Fact, it is more important for pastors and leaders to watch what they say and do more than church members. Pastor and leaders are held accountable to set a higher standard and to operate in a position of leadership—love, unity, and on a level of patience for those who are not where you are, but are trying to grow to get there. I am certainly not stating that pastors and leaders are perfect and that they each have no flaws and should operate perfectly. No so. No one is perfect but just as God has called you to the high level of position and responsibility you are holding, you are held to a high level of responsibility and accountability to do the very best that you can. You should pray and fast on a constant basis in those areas of struggle in-so-that you do not wound the flock *(the church members and others)*. This is the main reason why it was so important for Jesus to teach the disciples how to carry themselves in a Christ-like manner of holiness, unity, respect, love, and loyalty for others other than themselves or those who are familiar *(associate pastors, elders, ministers, family, friends, close clicks, etc.)* to them [Matthew 5]. Again, no one is perfect, so no one has the right to judge on any kind of level. We should pray for one another that he or she be healed and allow God to deal with the guilty party, not us.

If you are a person who holds pastors and leaders too high as if they are perfect, or put them on an impossible high level of standard that if they make one mistake, you cast them off the face of the earth, God has not called this. The bible states that *"he who is without sin, let him cast the first stone"* [John 8:7]. If you are a person who has never sinned since child birth <u>in thought and in deed,</u> go right now to your church or out into the world and throw your stone at someone as hard as you can... I do not believe there is one person who has the authority to that. No one can disagree with my words, especially when the Bible speaks that *"we all have sinned and fallen short of the glory"* [Romans 2:23]. We all are not called to judge. We are all called to pray.

Let's reach back to the example I wrote earlier. You may not have a story of attack as detrimental as Daniel's situation, but you have had a situation similar. **Document your story.**

Now that you have documented a little of what has happened to you, now take a moment to document what you did to heal from it. If any.

You may not have words to jot down because your hurt is still too sensitive and hard to express. You may still be healing or need help to heal from past attacks done against you in the church or outside of the church *(community outreach, missions, prison ministry, evangelism, etc.)*. I will do my best to help your healing process in this section by giving you some steps. If this fits you, use the lines below to first write down your experience or attack

Now write down your reaction to what they did:

Now write down the result of the attack:

Write how you overcame or how you got through it:

Write down your healing process:

Whatever your attack may be, I want to encourage you to forgive and to move on. As long as you are hurt, angry, and have put up a shield, your healing and peace will be pushed back. When you allow this process to be prolonged, you are giving your haters, enemies, attacker(s) the opportunity to have power over you. They have literally put you in a box or a place of bondage—bound to their negative power to keep you bound *(angry, afraid, hurt, in pain, place of unforgiveness, torment)*. God has a plan for your life and the place of defeat is not your home. It is time for you to release those who have hurt you deeply and move on with your life. It does not matter who they are, what position they hold or held, or how old or young they are, release them. I understand your hurt. I too was deeply hurt with the thoughts of "I don't ever want to see a church again." I understand how you can be so faithful in the church and your faithfulness not be good enough. I understand how you feel if you've ever been attacked by a pastor or leader in the church and they act as if they've done nothing wrong. I understand how it feels to be rejected in the church, feeling as if no one cares and no one's on your side. To do something wrong is one thing, but to be innocent is one of the hardest things to cope with as a result of an attack. One thing that helped me to heal is the words that God ministered to me as I sat on my bed of feeling defeated, alone, hurt, angry, and resentful. God ministered to me that **He was in control and that He would not put more on me than what I could bare**. He would show up and move on my behalf. I want you to know that God will do the same for you. He will show up and He will move. You are not accountable for them, but for yourself and for your actions. It is not for you to take action or to never go to another church or ministry. Do not slight or cheat yourself because of their negligence. Get in prayer as to what God would have you to do. Seek His direction through prayer and fasting. God is listening and He is ready to help you. He is ready to heal and to deliver you from those or that person(s) and what they have done against you.

It can be very challenging after you have been hurt or attacked in the church to go back in the sanctuary and see that person or those persons again. It is even more hurtful and damaging when they are the pastor or one of the leaders going forth during the service. I encourage you not to do something you will regret. Allow God to heal you and your situation. Only God can take vengeance and He is the only One Who can move in that situation. God is a God of love and order. As bad as your hurt may seem and I'm sure you are hurting, you must remember that God is a sovereign God and He is quick to forgive. As hard as it is for me to say this because of the sensitivity of your situation, I have to tell you the truth anyway. God wants you to forgive them and move on with your life. It is easy to hold them and want to see something detrimentally bad happen to them, to get back at them by stirring up verbal mess or a physical fight, or by controlling the situation by taking matters into your own hands by planning to do something physically harmful to them. It is not worth it. If you look at it, you have been guilty of something and you are not perfect. You have also sinned and regret some of the things you have done in your past. When thinking of it this way, it should make it easier to forgive them and move on with your life. Trust me, I'm a living witness. How you know that you have been delivered and healed, is when you see that person(s) and you do not have this rush of hurt or anger to build up inside of you to go give them a peace of your mind. Another instance is if someone mentions their name to you or in front of you and you do not frown or go off, then you know that you have been delivered and healed—you have released that person and can now experience a place of victory and freedom within. This is the goal of the Father. He wants you to be free and not allow people to put you in bondage or hold you in a box where you are so bound that you cannot get out. Freedom is on the way for you.

I can recall a time when I had just not too long had given my life to Christ and I so looked up to pastors and leaders in the church. During service I would watch them and look up to them and their position. I did this because I was trying to find my identity of what God had called me to do in the church. I looked up to them because it looked as if they had found their identity and calling and place of position in the body of Christ *(where God was using them)*. I too wanted that. I find this to be the case for many Christians who are young in Christ, their gifts, and/or in the ministry. I took on this attitude until after I had gotten involved in church ministry and became very active in several ministerial departments. One of which was on the clergy. God had called me into the ministry as an assignment to use me to preach the gospel, and to a place of intercessory prayer—among other departments. This is when the attacks began. The pastor and some leaders became very jealous of how God was using me and conspired against me. They told lies and believed lies from others who felt the same as they did *(their clicks)*. It was a hard time for me. I highly respected the pastors and all of the leaders in the church. This is when I realized that pastors and leaders were not perfect. The greater the promotion, the greater the attacks. The greater the anointing, the greater the attacks. The greater the level of faith, the greater the haters. God allowed me to go through this to show me that there is no one who is perfect and that He is the only One who is perfect and to look to Him and Him alone. Although God uses people to help mentor and lead others, He will never use them in a way that takes His place or to get you off of the purpose that He has called you to do. This is nothing to take away from them because they very well may be constantly praying about their struggle. I had to mature in ministry and in Christ. You have to mature in Christ and if you are active in ministry, you two have to mature and allow God to minister to you that there is no one who can take God's place; and no one is perfect as God is.

There is always a test in every attack. God will not ever allow you to be persecuted if He did not have something that He is trying to show or to help you with. He knows how much you can bear and He will not allow the enemy to overtake you. God is faithful and He will always allow you a way of escape [1Corinthians 10:13].

It Didn't Just Happen One Time

◊   ◊   ◊   ◊   ◊   ◊   ◊

THERE ARE SO MANY SHOCKING scenarios that happens in the church on a weekly basis. Many have literally brought wounded and damaged believers to a backslidden state. As a result, many have stopped being faithful to the local church. They have lost hope and these various scenarios have even caused them to question their faith in Jesus Christ, who they once strongly believed in. They felt as if God betrayed them and did not keep His Word to protect them.

> *Through these experiences it has helped me to grow and to see ministry assignment in a whole new perspective. I looked at serving God as serving Him in one place for the rest of my life, but He has allowed me to know that He had more than one place prepared for me.*

Before I give the scenarios, I have to share one of the detrimental experiences I had as a member of a local church in the past that almost made me never see another church in my life and end my life. I had worked faithfully in ministry for years at this local church. My main focus was to serve God and to stay faithful to Him, to the church, to leadership, and to the leader. Problems and clicks were the last thing on my mind especially due to the fact that it was not in my nature to neither cause trouble in God's house nor offend any of God's people. The first detrimental experience was a false accusation that a ministry leader went and lied to the pastor stating that I pushed her during church service in front of everybody. The pastor came to me and questioned me as if it was true. I could not believe that he would believe that person due to the fact that they had negative run-ins with others before and a problem with lying on others as well. It took me by such surprise that I did not know what the pastor or the so-called ministry leader was talking about. Then he had the nerve to have his wife in the office with us as if I was going to lie or get out of control. I was so deeply hurt because I thought he and his wife knew me by my Spirit *(the Spirit of God),* and that I had never had any prior negativities nor any run–in's in the church. I always respected them and stayed faithful doing what the pastor instructed me to do. I loved God so much that I wanted to please Him and serve to the best of my ability. Conflict was the last thing I struggled with. I love God's people and I love to see them happy. As a result of that situation, I informed the pastor that that person was lying and that I would never hurt anyone. As I spoke with them, the Lord was dealing with me and pressing in me that it was time to leave the church, but I kept fighting to stay.

The next detrimental experience came weeks after, this time with the pastor. I finally obeyed God and prepared to leave but had not told anyone, the pastor or the church. Nothing bad had happened which was the result of my leaving. I just wanted to finally obey God. I had previously made arrangements to meet with the pastor to let him know that I was leaving. During that meeting, he made a comment that changed my life. He told me that he was sitting me down, and for no apparent reason. I was shocked with disbelief. I asked him what did I do and he proceeded to say that he was not going to tell me the reason. I had never in my life heard of such. All I could think about was how faithful I had been in the church and was so faithful to leadership and had served faithfully, even when others did not. Also, when I knew he was not operating as a pastor should, I kept my mouth closed and just prayed. All I could think about was how could this person sit in front of me who is supposed to be the leader of the church have the audacity to come at me and throw false accusations at me and not tell me what wrong had I done. I knew it was the enemy. The devil was all over his face and at that point all I wanted to do was run out of his office and never come back again. I had met with him to leave the church anyway because God had already instructed me to do so, but this helped me to obey quicker. There was no trouble going on with me. I was never caught up in mess or drama. I always kept my mouth closed and prayed about all of the sins and evil mess the pastor was allowing from others in the church, while allowing them to still operate in various ministry positions. Before I walked in the office to tell the pastor I was leaving the right way, I wondered why God had told me to leave. But when I sat down in front of his desk I saw why. Right when I told him that I was leaving, he proceeded to say "that's too bad, I am sitting you down. You should have left before today. Now I am sitting you down…and don't come in the service crying." I was shocked and baffled for words and by his words. I was so hurt that I could hardly think. A pastor had never attacked me like that nor had I ever been told I was being sat down for no apparent reason. I thought, all the people he should have sat down, he was praising God with them on a weekly basis. All the evil that was going on in the church, he never met with them and sat them down. From that day on, it took a toll on me. I left out never wanting to see another church, nor another pastor, nor another so-called Christian again. As a result of this experience, I felt that God betrayed me and did not keep His Word. He let me down. He let them hurt me and get away with it.

At that time, I <u>could not see</u> that it was God pushing me to my next assignment and level. Although the attacks were from satan, God allowed them to come in order to push me to my next level. If they had not ever come, I would not have ever moved or obeyed. I would have stayed content. God spoke to me and warned me to move before the attacks came. He had been dealing with me about moving, but I was hesitant. I had gotten comfortable in the place I was in. So, God began to allow certain jealous ministry leaders to go to the pastor and spread lies along with the attacks from the pastor himself. Through these experiences it has helped me to grow and to see ministry and purpose assignment in a whole new perspective. I looked at serving God as serving Him in one place for the rest of my life, but He has allowed me to know that He had more than one place prepared for me. The greater was on the way and it could not be done there.

This happens all over the world. I have heard story after story and some are worse than my story. But I share this story only to minister to you and to encourage you if you are going through this or have gone through this type of attack. Certainly, I am not bashing any pastor or any church; whether they are right or wrong but the truth must be told. God has led me to share my story.

I want you to know that God has a greater level set up for you and it cannot be done in the place and position you are in right now. It is time to move and obey God. God's prophets, missionaries, and powerful men and women of God did not stay in one place for a long time in the Bible; they traveled and moved around doing the work and the assignment of the Lord. If you have been in a church for a long time with no thoughts or pressure to leave, it does not mean that it is time for you to leave. There are different levels, assignments and anointing's for different people. Your assignment may be to stay there but when or if God says move, obey His voice, pray, go on a fast, seek Him for direction and make arrangements to move. I did not move right away, so God permitted the enemy to team up on me with false accusations and lies in order to push me out. Do not get to this point where you run out instead of walking out.

Below, I want to give some shocking but true scenarios that happen in the church every day. These scenarios are wounding the Christian all over the world everyday:

- I was shocked he laid his hand on me and all I was doing was what the pastor told me to do.
- I was offended that she did not approve of my idea for the musical coming up, because she heard that I had just joined the church and felt that I didn't know anything.
- I get tired of going to church. There's no children or youth church so I'll just skip church and sell drugs on the corner.
- I hate church. I don't understand what the pastor is talking about I'm only fifteen years old.
- The pastor made a pass at me and I don't know who I can talk too. It didn't just happen once, it happened every time I went to church; until I left with the whole church against me because of rumors that I wanted the pastor, when it was the other way around.
- I've try so hard to fit in but every time I try to fit in, there are so many clicks that no one would welcome me and make me feel comfortable enough to fellowship with the body of believers.
- I dread going to church because when I get there, eyes are always on me and the way I dress. They can't wait to see what I got on to talk bad about me because of jealousy.

- I'm tired of them chattering and the laughing at my clothes just because they're not the styles that are in or the most popular ones.

- I have no money to be a part of almost all the ministry functions, and some of the church folks have the nerve to stick their noses up at me and not help, or act as if they don't even care.

- I hate when the pastor begs for a lot of money and make it seem as if the church is suffering, because the church congregation won't give when I'm unemployed and doing the best that I can.

- I tried to give my life back to God from coming back off the streets but when I walked in the church house, all the church folks looked at me crazy and start whispering against me. I've been a sinner all my life and I hated God, but when I made up in my mind that I was going to give God a try and become a believer and go to church, I was met by unbelievers that have been in the church for years talking against the God that I was trying to give my life too; so I quit and went back to my old self.

- I was in the church and my parents are devoted Christians and active in ministry. I decided to sing secular music and do my own thing in the world, but decided that the world meant me no good and went back to rededicate my life back to God and got active in ministry again. There were some so-called Christians who watched me from a far off, and looked at me crazy, and some even came in my face and had the nerve to ask me how can I come back in the church and sing the devil's music too. From that experience, I left the church and my parents did too.

These examples are some of what goes on in most churches. But most Christians will not be honest and tell someone for fear of what people may think about them, or for fear that they may be attacked and attempted to blame them for being the villain, rather than the victim. God is not pleased with this type of behavior in the church. When God first began to give Moses instructions on how to construct the tabernacle *(the church)* in the New Testament of the Bible [Exodus 25], He never intended for it to be a battle zone. His intentions were for His people to have somewhere to go to praise and worship Him, learn about His Word *(the Bible)*, and to believe in Who He is. The tabernacle *(the church)* was not just a put together thing, it was strategically designed by God in such a way that was to be regarded as a Holy place—a Holy atmosphere for God's glory. But when satan and sin got a hold of it, he began to bring all of his demons inside and began to set up kingdoms—kingdoms of lies through the lust of the flesh, the lust of the eyes, and the pride of life [1 John 2:16]. The church cannot continue to act in this way if it wants to be a successful church to do God's will and build a tabernacle that is pleasing in God's sight.

If you have been hurt by these examples that I previously have given, I want to encourage you by telling you to release it. Release all of the hurt, the trauma, the attacks, the residue, the bitterness, the anguish of soul, the hatred, the thoughts of murder, the retaliation, the "I'll never set foot back in that place again", and the "I'm gon' get em' all back attitude." I know this is the last thing you want to hear me say but I have to say it, **you must love and let it go**. Take note, I am not saying to let it go for their sake, but to let it go for your sake. See, you are not accountable for their actions; you are accountable for your actions. God holds you responsible for how you act and treat others. He will not punish you for something bad someone did to you or against you. He will deal with the enemy, but that is not your worry. You should pray and seek God for His love and comfort to saturate you, and to heal you so that you can move on with your life.

There is hurt and attacks that occur in every church. There is no perfect church. In fact, there is hurt and attacks everywhere. Don't you think the church will be attacked too? Of course, because it is the place of refuge, release and healing. It is the place where Christ is supposed to be. It is the answer to all of your problems, stress, and heartaches through receiving the Word of God. Jesus said that we would be persecuted [Matthew 5:20], but He would provide a way of escape [1 Corinthians 10:13], and he would also not allow you to suffer to be tempted above that what you can bear [1 Corinthians 10:13].

The doors of the church are closing more and more each day as the result of the Spirit of pride, which is so prevalent. Nobody wants to love like Christ loves. Every man for himself kinda' attitude. Everybody is fighting for all the wrong reasons, positions, and groups that God never intended for us to be fighting for. It is more important to try to get close to the pastor, the first lady *(pastor's wife)*, the ministerial staff, the clergy, the deacon board, the head musician, the most beautiful woman or most handsome man, than to draw close to the Lord. All minds, hearts, souls, and thoughts should be on the Lord while attending church. You should be so caught up in God's glory that nothing else matters. Nobody else matters. In fact, you should have this "My mind is on the things of God so get back devil" attitude. When your mind and focus is on the Lord, there is no room for stress, attacks, or drama. God wants all the glory. If you have or are a victim of any of the examples stated above, please allow God's healing to saturate you and heal you. I too understand your hurt. I was a victim of church hurt but now a victor. I had to allow God to heal my soul and restore me. I had to allow God to grow me up. I had given up on the church and the people in it. God ministered to me and let me know that He is still the church and that if I just focus on Him and not on people, I am safe from all of the hurt, drama, and attacks. I believe He can do this for you too. Be healed and let them go who have hurt you. You'll be glad you did. Trust me it's not for their glory and happiness, but it is for God's glory and the glory that will be revealed in you as an overcomer and a conqueror. Make up in your mind that you will not allow satan to even begin to think he has defeated you, kicked you out, or have stopped the plan and purpose that God has placed on your life. Don't give satan and your enemies the power over you. They are all gone on with their lives while you are still holding them and the hurt that they have done to you and against you. It is not worth it. Release them today in Jesus Name! Be healed in Jesus Name! Let it go in Jesus Name! Let them go in Jesus Name!

It is time for the people of God to pay attention to their actions in the church. Watch how you treat other Christians while doing your work in the church. Watch how you talk to others. Watch your tone and don't care attitude. There are thousands of wounded Christians and soldiers who were on the battle field for the Lord and was faithful in the church, but because of the lust of the flesh, lust of the eyes, and the pride of life operating in the leaders, they have pushed thousands of lay members out of the church. This is not the will of God. It is the plan of satan. The plan is to remove all of the powerful gifts and soldiers who are making a difference. We as Christians are obligated to love, esteem, help, to work, to praise and worship together, and to pray for one another. Division, control, strife, and jealousy are not a part of the plan. You may be saying, "I hear what you're saying but it didn't just happen once, it's happened over and over again and I don't know what to do." I encourage you to pray and turn it over to God. He will fix it. There is nothing too hard for God [Jeremiah 32:17]. Pray His Word over your situation or attack daily. It works only if you believe and have faith that He is able and will work it out for you. Without faith it is impossible to please God [Hebrews 11:6]. Without faith leaves no place for God to move in your situation, or even to destroy the attacks that you are going through. God operates only through your faith to believe. Although He allows us to cast our cares on Him because He cares for us, He still requires faith. You cannot talk faith—positive that God will move in your situation one day, and when the attacks strike again, you're downing God, your attackers, your church, or the situation you're in. **You must not be moved, this is faith**. I realize this is a hard thing to do in the mist of the attacks, battles, or detrimental situations, but you must do like Shadrach, Meshach, and Abed-nego did in the fiery furnace—**they were not moved**. They trusted God. No matter what came their way, they were determined that God would protect them and fight on their behalf; and that He did. Praise God for Jesus! Give it to God no matter <u>what</u> it is, <u>who</u> it is, or <u>how many</u> it is. It's worth it and God won't let you down. I'm a living witness.

The Hurting Closet—
Go Beyond the Closet Door

◊   ◊   ◊   ◊   ◊   ◊   ◊

- THE HURTING CLOSET
- MESSY CLICKS—SEXUAL RELATIONS—THE WAY OUT
- HAUNTED BY PAST PLEASURES—THE RELEASE
- CHURCH HURT BRINGS LEARNING EXPERIENCES
- THE YOUTH CHURCH HURT ENCOUNTERS
- CHURCH DRAMA

ITTING IN A DARK CLOSET CAN seem very dark, a little scary, very lonely and confusing. But yet, it can also feel as a safe haven from all of the stress, problems, and attacks you may be facing inside or outside of the church; and/or in your personal life.

> Once the sweet communion is in the forefront, then the channel is open for you to pour out your situations and concerns before Him—in His presence.

If you go and sit in that closet again, begin to realize that you are not the only one in that closet; and that there is a Greater One called Jesus Christ Who is in there with you, you will begin to feel a sense of comfort, peace and assurance that you are safe and that everything is going to be okay.

The closet can also be considered as a prayer closet or a get-a-way place. Whatever you want to call it, there is also another name that most Christians can identify with, which is, a place for the hurting Christian to pour out your every hurt or complaint to God. It is a place of worship and communion with God. It is a place where you can go behind the veil and release every secret, every hidden agenda, every scare, and every residue because Jesus Christ is in there with you. Try it. I challenge you to go in your closet. If you have one that you can walk in or sit in, cut off the light and sit down on the floor and began to talk to God. Imagine that you are at the Throne of God. Imagine that you are sitting at His feet. Imagine that you are wrapped in the arms of God and He is comforting you. You will quickly begin to feel His peaceful presence. You will quickly begin to feel His garment of love, healing, and deliverance. Whatever you need becomes the full focus of attention between you and God. He said in His Word, *"If you sup with me, I will come in and sup with you"* [Revelation 3:20]. God desires to sup with you. Meaning, He desires to come into your heart, mind, Spirit and soul; and commune with you. He wants to speak to you and tell you how much you matter to Him, how beautiful you are, how special you are, how important you are to Him, how much He loves you, how He longs to fulfill your needs, and to heal you from every hurt or challenge you may be facing. Nothing and no one should come between you and the presence of God that you feel.

Many times God only desires that you tell Him how important He is to you and how much you love Him and nothing else. He does not want you always ready to pour out all of your problems and cares on Him. There are times when He desires to visit/commune *(to sup)* with you and you alone without bringing others into His and your time with Him. Once the sweet communion is in the forefront, then the channel is open for you to pour out your situations and concerns before Him—in His presence. But make sure you do not leave His presence that way. You should always leave His presence with a faith of, thank You Lord that it is done. Thank You Lord that it is finished. Thank You Lord that it is well. I thank You Lord that You have heard my prayer and have answered me. Thank you Lord for Your Will being done. Then, lastly, began to worship Him with Thanks and admiration.

THE HURTING CLOSET

In His presence is where your hurt, pain, and shame are released in the Hurting Closet. God already knows why you're hurt, who hurt you, and how the situation came about. But He desires for you to release it to Him and let it go. Turn it completely over to Him and allow Him to work it out.

Hurt brings bondage. Bondage brings hindrance. Hindrance brings set-backs. You cannot go to your next level with hurt and set-backs. You cannot continue to re-live the actual act of the situation again and again. So it is best to release it and allow God to mend your hurt and broken heart back together again.

MESSY CLICKS—SEXUAL RELATIONS—THE WAY OUT

Many times Christians who have been hurt in the church have given up and their Christianity is questioned. Most church hurts come from sexual relations *[fornication, adultery, and homosexual acts]*, judgmental attitudes *[messy clicks and arrogant gestures]*, and unethical spoken words towards one another or towards the leader(s). As I have stated before, neither one of us have a Heaven or hell to put anybody in, as there are some Christians who think they can. What I love about God is the fact that if you have made mistakes in these areas, please do not live your life in condemnation, this is not of God [Romans 8:1]. We all have sinned and fallen short of God's glory. Just because your sin may not be as great or noticeable as others, does not mean that you are special and have no sin.

God is ready to heal you from people and worrying about what they think. **DO NOT WORRY ABOUT WHAT PEOPLE THINK.** You do not owe anyone accept God and the one you committed the sin with an explanation and/or repentance. I have learned by experience that people will try to put you in a box, and have control over you by hanging the sin over your head and keeping you isolated to a degree of depression, suicide, or even murder. God forbid. God will never hang your sin over you, but He will convict you not to commit the sin again <u>after</u> you have repented of the sin(s). The perfect example I can give which is found in the passage of scripture in John 4:7-28, about Jesus and the woman at the well. Jesus did not make the woman feel uncomfortable of all the men/husbands she was with, but he let her know to go her way and sin no more without condemning her. His conviction was that he encouraged her not to sin no more. He did not call her a dirty woman, whore, or even laugh in her face at the sins she was committing. Nor did He expose her and bring her business before the church as if to make a mockery of her. He was humble, sincere, and concerned about helping her to believe that he was Christ, knew the truth and for her to change. The church has no right to judge and aim to kick those who have made mistakes out of the church. Instead it, the church, is supposed to come together, embrace the sinner/struggling Christian, and pray together that they overcome the challenge they are having and be healed. The Bible say when you see your sister or brother overtaken in a fault, you who are Spiritual restore such a one in meekness, less you fall yourself [Galatians 6:1].

The church should not make backsliders, sinners, or even those who are faithful in the church who make a mistake feel as though they can never be forgiven. The church is not built to judge and to think of itself more highly than anyone. No one is exempt from the attacks of the devil. In fact, as I have stated before, the church is the first to be attacked because it is where the Body of Believers come together and conquer the forces of darkness and get the victory on a daily basis. It is a place where the Body of Christ should find God and God's presence. The devil hates God's presence. So if he can bring division in all sorts of ways, he will do it to keep the will of God from going forward, the people of God from gathering together, the Body of Christ from serving in unity, and the love of God shed abroad each time the church doors open; and also when there is a need among the Saints. The Bible says, one person will put one thousand demons to flight, but two or more will put ten thousand to flight [Leviticus 26:8]. If the church would come together and utilize their gifts in the great and power capacity that God has ordained, Christians can live a wholesome life free from sin on a daily basis by gathering together in sweet communion, love, unity, and truth. But this is not the case because of malicious slandering's, prying in others business, messy groupings, false accusations, busy bodying, itching ears, jealousy, strife, prideful attitudes and better than you looks, and so much more [Galatians 5:19-21]. Victory must come.

HAUNTED BY PAST PLEASURES—THE RELEASE

Over the years the church has been well known for relationships that start in pleasure but end up in horror stories. Pleasures have also occurred in the Bible. David and Bathsheba was one of them [2 Samuel 11]. When David first laid eyes on Bathsheba, he thought to himself he had to have her; and the fact that her beautiful profile didn't help either. The Bible says in verse 2 that she *"was very beautiful to look upon."* David could not live without the burning desire to have this beautiful woman. He went so far as to inquire about her and soon found out that she was married. But this did not stop him, he had to have her so that he had someone *[the messengers]* to go get her and he soon slept with her *[committed adultery]*. Sounds like the norm right? Well, she ended up getting pregnant [verse 4-5] and David later set her husband Uriah up to be killed [verses 6-21]. He wanted to get rid of him so that he could have her all to himself.

This same story happens in the church many times as the result of secret pleasures. You may have been involved in something such as this but maybe yours did not end up in murder or suicide, but it ended up in a heated fight, divorce; or maybe a custody battle. Pleasures in the church are normally not spoken of or exposed openly unless they are with a well-known senior pastor or leader. Most are hidden and the hurt of the secret pleasure burns within the two guilty parties, which lasts for a life time unless they release it. You may be a person who may have gotten caught up in a relationship like David's or something close to it. My mission is not to bring your past up or to open the closet of old haunted memories. We all have our share. But my mission is to help you by encouraging you to release it, close the door to it, and get your life back. You may have been involved in this type of situation or similar or even with someone who operates in the ministry *[the clergy—pastor, bishop, reverend, deacon, deaconess, or other]*. You thought that you would never end up in that type of situation in your life; and you are dealing with condemnation, feeling as though you cannot ever be forgiven, or even to be forgiven by your family or by the church. Can I be real for a moment? I have found that church people, not God's Saints, can be one of the cruelest people in the world. I have also found that most sinners will love a person who has made mistakes, because they understand how it feels to not be accepted and rejected. But Christians, especially God's people should be the ones who do not judge a person when they make a mistake and criticize them and spread their business all over the church. But they should help by listening, loving, forgiving, nurturing, and praying them back in God's Will again. Because of the church's slander, messy comments, evil looks, and abandonment, many who have committed this type of sin have fallen from the church roll and from grace. As I have stated before, if you have been involved in this type of sin and as a result you have been persecuted by the church you can be healed and there is still time for you to return.

You may be on the other end of the hurt—your husband or wife stepped out on you and you cannot find in your heart to forgive them and move on with your life. They may have even gone so far as to have a illegitimate child by the other person. I want to encourage you not to give up and to release the hurt, the shame of what people think, the hatred you have for your spouse, and to get your life back and move on. You owe no man an explanation but God and the person(s) involved. You and all the parties involved do not have to announce it to the whole world either. The only One you need to announce it to is God.

You may be the guilty party. I want you to know that God will forgive you immediately after you repent and release it to Him. Do not allow people, as I have been stating all through this book to have power over you. In fact, the very ones who are trying to control you by making you openly tell the truth or expose yourself, are the ones who may be secretly in a relationship themselves and do not know how to come out of it, so if they can keep all of the attention on you, their sins will be hidden and no one will ever know their dirt. But trust me, God does. And He will expose.

God will never embarrass you before the entire church congregation if you go to Him directly and ask Him for forgiveness, and turn away from that sin. He is not into making people look stupid or spotlighting them. He is into healing them. God loves you and He wants the best for you and your life, and to see you walking in wholeness and liberty through Jesus Christ. Allow today to be the day you:

1. Totally surrender your will by turning away from that sin.

2. Remove the guilt of what you did.

3. Remove the condemnation of feeling as though you cannot be forgiven or accepted again by God or those you hurt.

4. Release the embarrassment of what people think.

5. Get your life back and move on.

6. Walk in wholeness and liberty through Jesus Christ.

You may be one of the ones who have not ever told anyone and no one knows that you have been in an adulterous relationship with a man or woman, or of a same sex relationship; you can follow the points above and live a new wholesome life through Jesus Christ. You must forgive yourself. Most Christians who have been in these types of infidelity situations have a hard time forgiving themselves. God cannot work through hidden iniquity. You must release the hidden iniquity and allow God to come all the way in and do a cleansing and a total make over in you to a new life in Him. Amen? Praise God for the victory!

CHURCH HURT BRINGS LEARNING EXPERIENCES

Church hurt brings growth and learning experiences. I have learned this through my church hurt experiences. I have grown in more ways than one since the hurt I encountered with the church and leaders. God allowed me to learn from those areas of attacks and how to identify them in the future. At first I did not know how to identify them. I was looking at the pastor and other leaders as the enemy, but God allowed me to see that it was not them; it was the enemy operating through them to stop and to bring stumbling blocks in front of my purpose. I also learned not to hold pastors and leaders in such high standard and expected them not to behave in a negative unpleasing manner, and be ready to write them off when or if they did. God allowed me to know that they too make mistakes and are open to sin as well. The devil does not have a respect of persons who he chooses to use. He can use Christians as well as unbelievers to do evil. Please do not get me wrong, I was not looking to the pastor or to the leaders as Jesus Himself, but I held them in high standard because I felt that they should know better and should always watch what they do. But God allowed me to know again that they are not perfect and are subject to make mistakes as well as sin. I have grown and have learned not to ever hold any one in high standard to a degree that it puts them in the category of Jesus walking on the earth. Jesus stood alone. Nobody can ever say that they are Jesus. Nobody can ever say that Jesus sinned, though He was tempted, but He never sinned. Just as the pastor and leaders should lead with care, those that follow should follow with care, and with an open mind to quickly pray for them when a struggle or mistake is detected. Since my attack, the church *(a particular church I was a member of)* never called to embrace me nor did they ever try to reach out. There were a few that did, but there were many, many more that did not. The church must change. The Blood of Jesus is on the church. There is a covenant with the church. There is a mandate for every church to get it right. Jesus is coming soon and judgment will begin in the house of the Lord first *[the church]* [1 Peter 4:17].

Jesus is the greatest example of church hurt. He encountered so many hurts, persecutions, and attacks with church people and people in high rank, and so on. He never let His head hang low. He never gave up. Nor did He ever go and get revenge. Instead, He took it as a learning experience, forgave, stayed focus on His kingdom mission, purpose and assignment, and prayed and interceded for those who hurt, persecuted, and attacked Him. I realized that this is a tough pill to swallow especially if you are the victim. You may feel as though no one understands, love, or even cares. Trust me, I am with you; and I myself understands along with millions of others that are or was in the same position you are in right now. However, I have learned that you do not do it for the enemy; you do it for yourself and for your soul salvation. You do it for your healing, release, peace of mind, and strength to move on. God will do the rest. Just take one step at a time and allow God to take two behind your one step and watch your change come in miraculous ways day by day. God did it for me. It did not happen overnight. I had to take it one step at a time and day by day until God completely removed the hurt, pain, hatred, depression, lack of trust for the church, church people *(not Saints of God)*, and leaders. Now I am stronger, wiser, and able to discern and identify the traps and the snares of the enemy even more.

THE YOUTH CHURCH HURT ENCOUNTERS

Most people, mainly adults, do not talk much about young people when it comes to church hurt. However, we must realize that they are hurting too. In fact, they are hurting more than most adults. When I speak of young people, I am speaking of children, teens, and young adults from ages 5-35. They are going through some personal battles within yet they have no one to turn too or no one in the church that they feel that they can trust. Most churches do not have a children's church, youth church, youth ministry, or young adult ministry. As a result, either they are forced to listen to sermons that are way over their heads, or they turn to negative things and people outside of the church for the love, understanding, counseling, acceptance, and appreciation that is lacking where it should be granted. What they really need is the church. **It is important for all areas in the church to be covered.** If God has called you to a position of a pastor, please accept it with care and the fear of God. God will never leave a certain ministry out that is needed and beneficial for every area of the family and for the individual out. God has an utmost desire to draw everybody. God will never tell a pastor not to have a children's, youth, or young adult's ministry. Each of these ministries goes with all of the other ministries, such as, the men, women, and singles ministry; just to name a few. But most churches especially the smaller churches feel that since there are only two or three youths in the church, there is no need to establish that ministry because they do not have enough members. But this is not the will of the Father. It is God's will that these ministries go forth regardless. Jesus backs it up by saying, *"where two or three are gathered in His name, He promises to be in the mist of them [Matthew 18:20]."* God is with the young people no matter if there are only two or three children, youth, or young adults in the entire church just as He is with the adults. This is how the ministry grows. *"Youth begat youth."* They two will gather together as a ministry and go out and evangelize and tell other young believers or unbelievers in their schools or in their communities about Christ and about the church ministry. They will draw them in and this is how the ministry grows. As a result, this has taken a great effect on the younger generation in the church. With years of experience with working, counseling, and ministering to the children, youth and young adults, I have heard the most hurtful, heartfelt, touching stories and comments. I have heard their most deepest and inner cries.

These are some comments I have heard,

- "They're not enough things in the church for us to do. So we go out and find things to do, and people to associate ourselves with."

- Or, "I don't like goin' to church cause' tha' ol' folks think we don't know nothin' and think we all bad and we lazy, and they won't let us do nothin'. All we do is just sit in the pews and look stupid."

- Or, "I don't like to listen to the pastor cause' he talk to deep and I don't understand him/her."

- Or, "I don't like sittin' with my parents in church cause' they always think I'm not listening and always findin' somethin' to pick at me about."

- Or, " I don't like listening to the pastor cause' he always bashin' the young people like we all bad and gon' be nothin'."

- Or, "I want to be around other Christian youth, they are somebody I can identify with. But the pastor and the leaders don't let us get together cause' they think we always gon' do somethin' bad."

- Or, "I just got saved and I feel like I'm not growing cause' I don't have a youth pastor or leader that I can understand and Identify with to go higher in the Lord."

- Or, "can't no body in the church understands me or my problems. They all act too old."

- Or, "I need somebody to talk too cause' the pastor/leader keeps making a pass at me and I feel very uncomfortable around him/her."

- Or, "I got some real deep issues and I need somebody who is my age that I can talk too and counsel with, that is on my level and who's been through what I'm going through."

- Or, "I'm being molested in my home by my mother or father and I need to talk to somebody. But I there ain't no youth leaders available."

- Or, "All they do is bully me. I want to kill myself or somebody else."

And the list goes on and on and on.

These type of comments are real comments and have hurt me in such a way that I have made it a point to add them in this book in hope that a pastor or a leader will hear this, and learn from this and implement these ministries in their church ministry. It is imperative to hear the hearts of the young. Jesus said to the disciples "the greatest in the Kingdom of Heaven are those who become like a <u>child</u> shall enter the Kingdom of

Heaven, and those who receive a little <u>child</u> in Jesus Name shall receive Him [Mathew 18:1-5]. We must receive the young just as we receive the adults and ourselves. They are not to be put in a box away from everybody. They are not to be excluded and put in another room and not be used or made to feel as if they do not belong, are not saved, are not anointed, or are not needed. There should be a place for every believer in the Body of Christ who chooses to operate and be used in the church ministry. The entire family matters to God and should matter to the spiritual grow of every Christian family who desires to grow together in Jesus Name. We have heard the saying, "Every family that prays together, stays together." Well, I will add to that saying, "every family that worships and grows spiritually together, will always have the Lord as the center of the family and over the entire house."

CHURCH DRAMA

The church must not preach or yell at the young people. Instead, it must be willing to walk with them through their mess and mistakes just as someone did when you were young and your mess of mistakes. You as a parent and the church should discipline and then love, forgive, understand, listen and lead them the right way. I will give you a perfect example, in John, chapter 18, verses 10-11. Peter cut off the right ear of the high priest as Jesus quickly disciplined him by saying, *"Put up thy sword into the sheath: the cup which my Father hath given me, shall I not drink it?"* Jesus was disciplining Peter for doing what he did. But He did it in love. Jesus also did not give up on Peter or cast him away because of his mistake, He told him to put his sword back in its place. In other words, he was telling Peter not to do what he did. We as adults and more seasoned Saints of God should be the same as Jesus. We must help and discipline our young people in this same way when they make a mistake. We must teach them and explain what they did was wrong with love, and love them and forgive them as we continue to lead them.

Without any plans in place to implement this ministry in the church, the church wonders why young saved and holy Ghost filled people have turned away from the family, God, and have left and are leaving the church. They do not want to listen to any Christian music, a Christian pastor/leader, the church, their parents/family or even have a heart to love and to follow God.

They are simply not taught in the church and are pushed to the back of the church, or in another room to play games with no biblical teaching or love shown toward them. Like a daycare. This should not be so in the church. This brings church hurt and scares for life.

There are more important things happening in the church other than getting off on finding out other people's or young people's sins, and exposing them is their ultimate goal. There is not enough time to drive down everybody's street, into their personal lives and try to expose them, or try to make them feel worse than they already feel; while at the same time not recognizing that you offend your brother or sister every time the church doors open. There is no sin greater than the other. God is no respect of persons [Romans 2:11], He sees sin all the same. A little white lie is the same as a huge white lie. A small sin is the same as a huge sin. But because a person may be in power and feel as though they cannot be removed, or as though no one can check or be rude to them, they go around the church treating others unkind and wounding them from either getting involved in the church ministry or activities. As a result, they leave the church, or even to the degree that they never see another church again in their life. Church members all across the globe must constantly watch how they treat one another in the church. While no one is perfect, we all must strive on a daily basis for perfection and shun from anything that looks, sounds, or smells like drama in the church.

Church Conflicts can ruin a church that is standing for the Lord. This is the devil's goal. The church must be strong and stand together as a cohesive and rid out anything that will bring conflict against the clergy, leaders, each ministry, members, the Will of God or against the vision of the church that should only be from God.

God's true presence from His Holy Spirit should be the ultimate focus while our time is spent in the church. We must seek the Heart of God constantly for direction, guidance, how we must come off, where to be used by God, what to say, and what to do. For example, just because you may like to sing may not be God's Will for you to join the choir ministry. You must seek God's direction and leading and find out where you belong and what your purpose is at that particular church. If every Christian would take time to do this and not move until they receive an answer from God, the church would run smoother, peaceful, loving, drama free, and without a press to get involved in various ministries. Everyone would operate in their anointing at ease with less conflict.

Below is a pie chart that shows how the church should be set up in terms of the believer as he, she, the family, the child, and the teen is supposed to be set up:

GOD

SENIOR
PASTOR

CLERGY/ MINISTRY
LEADERS

STAFF/VOLUNTEER
WORKERS

CHURCH FAMILY

If every person finds his or her place and stay in your place, the church will run smooth in the order it is designed to run. This should be a goal for every church every day.

The Binding and Loosing Closet

◊   ◊   ◊   ◊   ◊   ◊   ◊

ATTHEW 18:18 IS A KEY SCRIPTURE for binding and loosing the enemy's attacks. It states, *"whatsoever you shall bind on earth shall be bound in heaven: and whatsoever you shall loose on earth shall be loosed in heaven."* Just as I have explained "The Hurting Closet" in the previous chapter, it works the same with this chapter. The only difference is, your focus now is praying specifically against the forces of darkness *(all of your enemies who hurt you in or outside of the church, or in your personal life)*. You are still in full

> *When you bind, that immediately stops any attack against you. When you loose, that immediately releases all the angels in Heaven to move on your behalf according to your need.*

fellowship with God and you are still imagining through faith that you are still sitting at His feet with His arms wrapped around you, but this time you are quoting scripture of faith to your hurt, pain, attacks, and situation. You are literally praying that God would move, heal, and deliver those who have and/or are hurting you. Do not pray in anger or in hurt. Having that in your heart will not allow God to move for you.

You must release the hurt, anger, and inner iniquity. Trust me, God knows when you are still angry and hurting. He knows everything. Once you release this, then you can release everything and receive your full deliverance and healing. By refusing to do this, you are giving the enemy *(those who hurt you)* full power over your mind, actions, attitude, and lack of ability to worship God to the fullest. I'm a living witness. During the time I was hurting and angry from the hurt of people who hurt me in the church, I could not receive my full healing, deliverance, nor could I tap into God's presence to worship and praise Him effectively. As much as I tried, and the more I tried to press through it, it would not work. God spoke to me and said, *"release the hurt and then I can come in."* I begin to cry out and ask God to heal me from those who hurt me, and begin to stand on Matthew 18:18. God encouraged me through His Word that He has given us full authority over the enemy and by faith. We have the ability to bind *(refuse, rebuke, not accept)* the enemy on earth and he will be bound in Heaven. And whatever we loose *(bring into existence, receive, open up the channel)* on earth will be loosed in Heaven. This is the binding and loosing closet.

By faith this can happen immediately the more you make a conscious decision to release and know it's not worth holding on to. I encourage you to know who you are and that you have full power over the devil *(your enemies, those who hurt, wounded, or have scared you).* As I was reading God's Word, I came up on the passage of scripture where Jesus was encouraging the disciples to love their enemies and pray for those who despise, abuse, and hurt them (Matthew 5:43-44). I realize this is a hurting and touchy scripture especially if you are still being hurt and abused or it is still fresh because it just happened. You honestly feel as if your enemies should be healed and not you. You feel that it is because of them which is the reason why you're hurting. You feel as though you are hurting too much to forgive and to pray for them. I want to encourage you again. You are not doing it for them you are doing it for yourself. You are doing it for your peace and freedom. God desires that you be loosed from them so that He may come in. The Blood of Jesus washes away hurt and pain. You must apply the Blood of Jesus over your mind and emotions on a daily basis so that you will not go back. The Blood allows you to love your enemies even when you do not think it is possible. I can tell you by experience today that it is possible.

You must know the power that you have in Jesus. The Word of God is power and brings power to any situation that you are facing. When you bind, that immediately stops any attack against you. When you loose, that immediately releases all the angels in Heaven to move on your behalf according to your need. It is important to be specific but according to God's Will and not your fleshy Will. You cannot try to get back at the devil *(your enemies)* on your own. You must allow God to do it. God is not a demon nor is He about confusion. He wants us all to get along and live in harmony with one another. It is not His Will that Christians fuss and fight, hate and back bite, or be jealous of one another, this only leads to division and a detrimental environment. God is peace and this is what you should always strive for.

Sheltered Within—
The Retaliation Process

◊   ◊   ◊   ◊   ◊   ◊   ◊

HEN A SOLDIER ON THE BATTLE FIELD is wounded, the first thing that soldier does is quickly find a place of shelter. He or she closes themselves off from the enemy so that they will not wound them again. They quickly begin doctoring on their wounds as they cry out for help. They do not want to continue to fight. They do not want to laugh and have a casual conversation. All they want to do is get help for the problem(s) that they are currently facing at that moment. This is the same thing that happens when a

> *Allow God to remove the stronghold that was caused through hurt and anger. Your health is in jeopardy if you do not let it go, forgive and allow God to heal you from within.*

Christian or a lay member in a church is wounded. They close themselves off from everybody and become sheltered within. Depression is sheltered within them. Bitterness is sheltered within them. Hurt is sheltered within them. Hatred is sheltered within them. Anger is sheltered within them. Unforgiveness is sheltered within them. All of these things and more are very dangerous and can cause a person to do something deadly or harmful to themselves or to others. If this is you I am talking to, please do not resort to something deadly or harmful to yourself or to the person, or persons who have hurt you; and have caused you to become sheltered within. Jesus never died on the cross for your sins and mine for you to give up and allow the devil to make you do something that you will live to regret. Jesus died for the hurt you are dealing with. He understands your hurt. He too was persecuted for righteousness sake. But He did not quit or give in, He hung in there because of the Kingdom purpose, Kingdom assignment, and Kingdom promise. There is a promise and a reward for you if you do not quit and do not do something detrimental to yourself and to others. Again, as I have stated before, God will take care of your enemies or those who have hurt you [Psalms 37:1]. He is not asleep, He is yet alive and is listening to your every petition. He is drying your every tear. His precious Holy Spirit is wrapping His arms around you and is comforting you. His everlasting love is moving within your heart. He has caught every tear you've cried and has felt every groaning or soul you have yelled out. He is fighting for you. Be comforted and know that God will not let you down. I know it gets hard sometimes and it seems as if God is nowhere to be found in your storm, but He is there and He is listening, and He will come through for you.

God can deliver you and set you free from any thoughts that make you want to retaliate and do or say something that you will live to regret. He says in 2 Corinthians 10:4 that the weapons of our warfare are not carnal, but they are mighty through God to the pulling down of strongholds—strongholds of fear, anger, depression, hatred, retaliation, and suicide. Allow God to remove the stronghold that was caused through hurt and anger. Your health is in jeopardy if you do not let it go, forgive and allow God to heal you from within. Hurt and anger brings stress and stress brings an unhealthy body such as, heart attacks, strokes, cancer, diabetes, etc. Release it today and live a wholesome free life of love, forgiveness, and peace in Jesus Christ.

I am going to give you some real life scenarios to help you identify when you have been battered and sheltered within. After these scenarios, I am going to show you how to obtain the retaliation process the right way.

REAL LIFE SCENARIOS WHICH CAUSES A PERSON TO SHELTER WITHIN:

1. You are a victim of spouse abuse. Your spouse beats you every day over everything they can think of. You two are pastors, or leaders, or active members in the church. The last thing you want is anybody to know about your suffering and deteriorated relationship. So you try to go on with the false happy face as if all is well.

2. You are a victim of adultery. Your spouse has stepped out on you and has told you that he or she is in an infidelity relationship with another man or woman. They have requested a divorce and have moved out of your house. You two are either co-pastors of a church, deacons or very active leaders in the church, or faithful church members.

3. Your husband or wife, in which is a pastor or leader gets murdered or commits suicide and you are forced to take over the church.

4. The pastor, leader, or someone in the church sexually touched you and you do not know how to tell anybody. You have literally given up on the church and have closed the door to your dark room, and have made up in your mind that you are not coming out to let anyone hurt you again. Your room if full of depression with no sign of life. Coming out of the room is a struggle.

Answering the phone is a struggle. All you can think about is what they did to you.

5. You got caught up in a fornicated relationship with someone outside of the church and the entire church found out about it and now you do not want to be active because of fear of what people say and think. All you can think about is the mistake you made, and the pain of the embarrassment of what people said or say about you.

6. You may not have done anything wrong and are a victim of lies and false accusations. Retaliation seems to be the best choice. You have planned it out in your mind of how you're going to get them back through anger.

7. You are struggling with a homosexual relationship and the people in the church have come up with a conspiracy against you and have voted to stop you from getting involved in the ministry and to put you out of the church.

8. Your past holds many skeletons—prison time, gang banging, bullying, juvenile delinquency, or even had a baby out of wedlock. You have been delivered but everybody at the church knows your past and always reminds you of it—ready to put you down, or stares at you while snickering to others about it, or goes and tell the pastor or associate pastor lies about something you did which was not true.

9. You are an unemployed single dad or mom, the dad or mom walked out on you and left you with kids to raise on your own. You asked the church for help but they refused to help.

10. You had a baby by the pastor who is married and the pastor does not want to support, or want anything to do with you, and wants you to keep the baby quiet.

As you have read over these real life scenarios, one or more of those may be your situation. I want to encourage you not to retaliate physically. I want to help you to retaliate the right way through the retaliation process.

THE RETALIATION PROCESS:

Jesus is best known for how He retaliated against his enemies and those who set themselves out to hurt Him. He retaliated through His love, will to win, will to overcome, will not to allow the devil to see Him sweat, and the will to get to the place of why He came and to fulfill it. You must do just as Jesus did. I realize it is hard for you right now, but not many are going to do it for you. They are not going to have a pity or defeated party with you, nor are some going to want to see you win. You must get up off of your bed of affliction, bed of depression and anger. You must tell yourself that you are going to win and refuse to be defeated by the attack of the devil that attempts to bring set-backs. Set-backs are set-ups. You have been set-up for your breakthrough today if you want it. Do you want it? I know you do. I realize this is very hard but you can do it. It is like a coach pushing his or her athletes to win. I am pushing you not to give up and to go on with your life and win. The devil does not want you to win nor does he want you to get your full freedom in Jesus Christ. He wants you lay down and die and give up, suffer a stroke or even a massive heart attack; and not fulfill your God given purpose. What I love about God is that He comes when everybody has given up on you and you have nothing and nobody left. He will never quit on you. He loves you no matter what mistake you may have made, or through your most hurtful moment.

As I have stated before that I am a living witness of being lied on, pushed back, rejected, talked about, hated on, called holy roly because of my faithfulness and love to God, jealous of the anointing on my life, being hurt by a pastor, and so on. So I do understand and I can stand here as I write this book and tell you that you can overcome it and be healed from the pain of your past and from all of those things that has happen to you and against you.

Sheltered within is the result of feeling like a failure from the pain of your past and from hurts that was not your fault. When a person has been hurt it can cause that person to close up, over eat, lean toward the same sex—receiving everything they wished from the opposite sex, having threats and thoughts of suicide, refusing to marry or to marry again thinking that no one can make you happy, or fear that they will not meet your standards.

There are three ways to overcome and receive victory:

1. Look to Jesus for help (2 Samuel 22:4, 7).
2. Shut out what people say (Proverbs 30:8).
3. Move on with your life (John 8:36).

The Shelter of God's Love

◊   ◊   ◊   ◊   ◊   ◊   ◊

OD'S LOVE IS NOT ONLY A FEELING, it's an experience that anyone dealing with church hurt or any type of hurt or pain, can be healed through Christ's love. Jesus went through church hurt. In [John 2:13-17], he was so angry at the church folks for committing usury *(selling and exchanging goods in and out of the church).* He was so angry that the bible says that He began to tear up what they were trying to sell and begin to turn over

> *The shelter of God's Love protects you from any hurt outside of it. When you do your work as unto the Lord it does not matter if you are acknowledged.*

tables. Although He had this experience, He still had love for the people. His love never changed. This is why I say love is not just a feeling, it is an experience. You may have had an experience in the church that you are not proud of or dare not to talk about. Remember, God is the only One you owe an explanation and repentance to. No one on this earth have a Heaven or hell to put you in. God is the only One who is capable, able and ready to forgive you of your sins, hurt, anger, and disappointments. People are not capable of giving you what only God can give. This is why you should only ask Him to heal you. You should tell your inner most secrets to Him. You should lay everything that you are dealing with at the altar. God is ready to shower you with His love. Be healed today and start a fresh and new life as a new person in Jesus Christ, Who is ready to conquer each day with a completely new attitude, determination, and victory—faith filled Spirit.

The shelter of God's Love protects you from any hurt outside of it. When you do your work as unto the Lord it does not matter if you are acknowledged. It does not matter if you are appreciated. It does not matter if you do not get one thank you. It does not matter if they take the credit that belonged to you and give it to someone else. It does not matter what people say negatively about you. **The only thing that matters is the fact that God acknowledges, appreciates, credits and loves you.** He will reward you openly [Matthew 6:18]. The only thing that should be on your mind is pleasing the Lord. Where Christians get in trouble is when we start fixing our minds on people instead of on the Lord. When your mind is on the Lord, when attacks come up against you, you will not be moved. It is a hard place to get to for most people, but it is a safe, peaceful, and rewarding place.

God's love over shadows hurt, pain and defeat. God's love brings brotherly love through kindness, unselfishness *(knowing it is not all about you)*, and the ability to be a peacemaker in the mist of every storm or conflict. God's love heals all wounds—deep and shallow. God's love helps you to love and to forgive when crisis come that is not your fault. Without love, nothing you do matters. Without love, nothing matters.

Experiencing God's love brings a life changing experience that changes your life forever. You may have been abused, God's love will heal and help you to overcome. You may have been in a state of depression for years and coming out seems impossible, ask God for His love to over shadow you and fill you. The greatest gift is love [2 Corinthians 13:13].

God gave His only begotten Son for the remission of sins. That is love. If God can give His only son, you can love through any obstacle or situation that you may be facing or have faced in life [John 3:16].

Love conquers all fear. It sees no fear, it sees no wrong. It does not dwell on fault finding and hurt. It looks for ways to overcome. There is a point and a time in your life when you must do a reality check and say to yourself, you will not hold those who have hurt you any longer, and you will choose to release them and allow God's love to shelter you and to heal you. It is like doing a self-evaluation check. It is time for Christians to check themselves by holding up their own mirrors and evaluate what's really going on inside. No more pointing the fingers. God's love is much too great and can penetrate through anything and anyone who desires it.

You may be facing so much pain to a degree that you just want to give up and end your life. The church was so cruel to you and you want to give up. I encourage you not to make that your decision. You are a strong person and you can make it through this time in your life where you feel as though no one loves you or cares. God loves you and He knows what you are facing and feeling. He knows what they did against you and He is ready to listen to you and make it better for you. Nobody can make it better like Jesus can. He is waiting, willing and ready for you to give it over to Him so He can fix it for you.

You are a winner. You must chose today that you are going to win against the fight of the pressure you are facing, and not allow the enemy to hold you captive in the bondage of hurt, fear, and pain. It only wants to keep you down so that your purpose will never be fulfilled. We as Christian believers win in every situation because God's love helps us. We do not lose or allow someone to have power over us in-so-that we lose our faith to live on, believe in God, and the power to overcome. God's love fights back on our behalf and wins that fight against the fight of suicide, depression, oppression, abuse, and I will even go so far as to say murder. I encourage you to win and experience God's love today and everyday pf your life.

Letting the Pain Go

◊　　◊　　◊　　◊　　◊　　◊　　◊

WE HAVE ALL BEEN WOUNDED AT ONE point in our lives. I can remember a time as a little girl riding my bike down a sidewalk and coming to a huge hole as a result of the city doing major construction work. The hole was so large that a car could fit down inside of it. Glass and debris was scattered everywhere inside of it. A group of kids and I ignored the construction site and warnings, and all of the glass and debris that was everywhere; and started jumping a ramp made by one of the kids with our bikes as we attempted to jump over the huge

> *I understand you're hurt because I've been there. I have been deeply hurt by jealous pastors and leaders who made it their point to see me hurt...*
>
> *...God has a purpose for everything, even when you may not see it, agree with it, or even understand it. He is working something in you and working everything out for your good.*

gigantic hole with our bicycles. Fortunately they made it across, but unfortunately I did not. I ended up falling into the gigantic hole with all the glass and debris and as a PAINFUL result; I cut my hand deeply and needed stitches. This was a terrible pain that not even medication was able to cure. I needed something greater. Although I tried very hard to remove the pain myself through my own strength, I still could not remove the excruciating pain on my own. As I share this true story, I am saying to you that it will take God who is the greatest pain medication that anyone could ever have. He is the only One who can wipe away the deep rooted hurt and pain that you are going through. He is the only One who can go deep into the crevasses of your heart, mind, body, and soul and heal and deliver you to make you whole. Just as I tried to let the pain go, I could not let it go on my own; I had to allow God to remove it. So, I say to you today, let the pain go by asking God to remove it because it is too great for you, and I assure you that He will.

I understand your hurt because I've been there. I have been deeply hurt by jealous pastors and leaders who made it their point to see me hurt. These were men and women in great and small positions of power and authority in the church. It was hard listening to them preach the Word of God and then almost immediately after, be crucified and persecuted falsely. It was an unbearable time for me because I loved and respected them and did them no harm but was only trying to be faithful in the call that God had assigned me to and to do the will of God. I was at a "I give up state." It took every bit of God to help me realize at that time that they were still in the flesh *(this earthly body)*, and they were still capable of making mistakes. Although that was no excuse for their actions, unethical ways, and persecutions against me, God allowed me know that I needed to let the pain go, and forgive them and move on with my life. I could not remove the hurt myself, it took God removing it from me which allowed me to eventually forgive and move on with my life.

Everything happens for a reason. Romans 8:28 tells us *"...that all things work together for good to them that love God, to them that are called according to His purpose."* God has a purpose for everything, even when you may not see it, agree with it, or even understand it. He is working something in you and working everything out for your good. He is taking you to another level and therefore He may choose to allow you to be treated in the way you are or were treated in order to make you strong in trust and faith in Him. See, when you are trusting in God, because He cannot lie through His Word, He will not allow you to be trampled over by the enemy. It may not look like it at that moment, but trust me, they are not or did not trample over you. At that time, I did not want to hear anything from anybody who was not on my side to understand my hurt. But now that I have been healed from the hurt and accepted the fact that it is my past that came to push me into my destiny. Still it doesn't justify their evil unethical actions and persecutions against me. God allowed it because He knew that I would trust Him no matter what and to see the salvation of the Lord. If this is you and you are currently going through this pain, I encourage you to release it and let it go. God cannot heal you beyond your faith to believe that you can be healed. You make a conscious decision that you are not going to continue to give your enemies power over you through hurt, and let them go by releasing them to the Lord. God's Word tells us to fret not ourselves of evil doers, neither be envious of your haters/enemies, for soon they shall be cut off [Psalms 37:1]. God encourages us in Psalms 37:7 to rest in the Lord, and wait patiently for Him to move on your behalf; and fret not yourself as it may look like they are prospering in their way, because they are not. Remove your anger [Psalms 37:8] and let go and let God heal. Their time will come and they will reap what they have sown [Galatians 6:7]. You should pray for them, and bless them for it is God who takes vengeance not us [Matthew 5:44]. I know this is the hardest thing to do, but I encourage you personally that you can do it. I had to do it. The same person(s) who hurt me in the past came across my path years later and I was able to hug and speak to them as they spoke to me. I hugged and spoke to them as if they never did anything against me. I knew then that I had released them. I knew then that I had released all the hurt that they had ever caused me. I did not do it for their good, I did it for my good. I realized that I could not enjoy the full life of freedom and wholeness in Jesus Christ if I continued to hold all that hurt and anger. I realized that I was hurting innocent people, family and friends around me at that time because I was unconsciously and unknowingly acting out; and taking the hurt and anger out on them—which was not right. I also realized that stress, hurt, and unforgiveness brings sickness, but through my trust and faith in God to let the pain go, He took it away because I allowed Him to. Again, it is a conscious decision. You have to make up in your mind that you do not want to hurt anymore. You have to make up in your mind that you will not hold all the anger anymore. The one(s) who have hurt you are long gone on with their lives and you are still holding all of that in your heart, mind, and spirit. It is not worth it. You are allowing them to have power over you. You are putting them in control of who you are and how you act or what you say; which always is not a person that is good to be around. I am not a super woman, my healing did not happen overnight. It was a process. There are times when some can just let it go quickly, but there are also times when others take longer. Both are good as long as you are making progress. Process is progress as long as you are looking up to the Lord for healing, help, and assurance that He will complete His work in you.

I encourage you today not to give up and to make today your day to **LET THE PAIN** go and get your life and freedom back from the devil who stole it in the first place. Know in your heart and through faith that God will never fail you [Deuteronomy 31:6]. He will come through for you because He cares for you [1 Peter 5:7]. He sees what you are going through and have been through. He remembers the labor of love you have given and have shown [Hebrews 6:10]; and He has not forgotten about you. He sees how faithful you were in the church and to leadership. He is not ignoring you. He never sleeps nor does He ever slumber. Your time and your day will come. Better yet, I will go as far as to say that your reward is on the way, but first you must release all the pain and let your haters/enemies go. Amen? Amen. God bless you. You can do it. I'm praying for you.

You may be saying, Stephanie I just can't release it on my own. I'm so hurt and so mad that I can't even pray. Well, let me help you. Just say from your heart, and in faith, the prayer I have provided for you below. Pray *(say)* this prayer daily until you feel a release in your spirit and know that your healing has manifested:

> *Father, I know You are the God of the universe. There is no one greater than You. Therefore, I believe there is nothing too hard for You to accomplish. I realize that You are the God that can heal us from anything. Isaiah 53:5 confirms that you were wounded for my transgressions, You were bruised for my iniquities, the chastisement of our peace was upon You, and because I trust Your Word and know it to be true, by your stripes I am healed. I believe this by faith and from this day forward I am healed, set free and made whole from hurt and anger _____ in Jesus Name, Amen.*

As you have prayed *(spoke)* the prayer above in faith and belief, know today that you are healed, set free and made whole from hurt, pain, and the anger from your enemies. Now you can go on in Jesus Name and live a life of freedom and fulfill the purpose that He has placed on your life to fulfill. Get back in a faith, bible based church. Don't go in afraid and overly sensitive. Don't go in ready to judge everybody. There is no perfect church. Say your prayer before choosing a church, wait on God's answer, and choose the church that He leads you to connect with. Get active in a ministry that He leads you to. Stay faithful to the work of God and may the Lord always be with you is my prayer. God bless.

Below, verbally speak this morning prayer confession of faith over your life on a daily basis until it becomes a part of your life and you see manifestations happen:

> *Lord, I thank You for dying on the cross for my sins just as John 19:30 tells me. Therefore I thank You for the forgiveness of my sins today and I ask that You will be the center of my day today. Holy Spirit lead, guide and direct my plans on this day. I thank You that no hurt, harm, danger, attacks, demonic activity, or sickness shall come near me or my mind and body. I plead the Blood of Jesus Christ and I thank you that I am free from sin and the guilt of shame and that I live a life of peace, love for myself and others. In Jesus Name, Amen.*

The Complete Release
& Restoration Process

◊　　　◊　　　◊　　　◊　　　◊　　　◊　　　◊

A S I HAVE MENTIONED IN THE PREVIOUS chapter that healing from hurt or church hurt does not always happen overnight. It is at times a process, but God is faithful. He will heal you and help you to move on.

THE COMPLETE RELEASE:

Complete release is total freedom. When you completely release the hurt or whatever your situation is, it is gone and it will not ever return unless you allow it to. Just as you made a conscious decision to release it all, you can make a conscious decision to allow it to

> *There is no hurt or pain too great for God to heal and restore...*
>
> *...You cannot heal yourself. It's too great. You cannot handle it...*
>
> *...He is the healer of all the drama that you are going through or went through...*

all return. You must make up in your mind that you are going to stay completely free from church hurt, any hurt or anger that has had you once bound. **It is a terrible thing to be bound and not know how to get free from it.** It is just like being a victim to someone binding you with a rope tied in a tight knot—tied in such a way that your release is impossible. You are a prisoner to that person(s) or thing. They have complete control over you. They can make you laugh, cry, yell, fight, or whatever they want to do with you. What an awful position to be in. To you it would seem as if you are going to be bound forever because the stronghold or the bondage to hurt, anger, bitterness, unforgiveness is much too great to break out of. But I know a God that specializes in loosening the knotted robe that have you bound. He will set you free but you have to completely and totally release it. This does not mean let it go temporarily and when the hurt makes you angry again pick it back up. No this way is useless and it is not the Will of God for your life. God wants you to enjoy your life and letting the devil know he's defeated, giving God all the glory.

THE RESTORATION PROCESS:

Restoration means to be restored. To go back to who you are—who God made you to be as He formed you before you were in your mother's womb [Jeremiah 1:5]. There is no hurt or pain too great for God to heal and restore. Note that I am saying process again. Well, that is what I mean. I have encountered various people in my life time that have been deeply hurt and tried to get free on their own and by their own strength. I want you to know that this process is not healthy. You cannot heal yourself. It's too great. You cannot handle it. It may seem as if it's working at first, but as time goes on there will be someone and something else that will hurt you and make you angry and take you right back where you were in the very beginning. God allows this to happen to show you that you need Him and that you cannot make it without Him, nor can you heal yourself without Him. He is the Healer. He is Healer. He is the Healer of all the drama that you are going through or went through. You have to know in your heart, mind, spirit, and soul how powerful and mighty God really is. He is greater than you can ever imagine. He can do what seems impossible to you. It is possible to God. Praise God! Aren't you glad you serve a God like that? I sure am. There was a time when I did not know Him and had no knowledge of how great He really is, but through my confessing and accepting and receiving Him into my heart, mind, and soul, I became his child. He was waiting for me. He always had a special place in Heaven waiting for me behind His veil of Glory, ready to bless me with whatever my need was and still is today. He can do the same for you as you completely release and allow the restoration process to begin through God's precious healing. Will you trust Him today? Will you allow God to heal you? Will you completely give your problems, hurt, pain, anger, and so on to God, and be totally free today in Jesus Name? Praise God! I agree with you in prayer today and by faith I thank Him for your complete healing and release today! Amen.

Just Do You

◊　　　◊　　　◊　　　◊　　　◊　　　◊　　　◊

- LET EM' TALK
- DO NOT ALLOW PEOPLE TO PUT YOU IN A BOX
- STAY IN YOUR PLACE

GOD CREATED YOU JUST THE WAY YOU ARE. Nobody can be you nor can they successfully imitate you to the fullness. They may come close, but they will never be able to completely be who you are. God created each person differently in their own unique way.

The church has grown to a fashion statement over the years. Everybody tries to either outdo one another by the way they dress, look, or try to keep up with one another. There is nothing wrong with wanting to look good,

> *God created you just the way you are. Nobody can be you nor can they successfully imitate you to the fullness.*

but when it begins to take your attention away from God's presence and getting what you need from Him, it becomes a problem. It also becomes a problem when you think its all about you and you are all of that.

I have seen people/Christians judge other people/Christians by what they look like on the outside when in fact they were a totally different picture on the inside. God never designed humans to try to copy one another. He <u>specially, carefully, and specifically</u> designed each one of us in a unique way that highlights his or her own self. It is important to tap in to what God made you to be, what He made you to do, what He made you to look like, and who He made you to become. In 1 Corinthians 7:19-24, it speaks of just being yourself. I say **just do you**. If you were a prostitute when God found and changed you, or you were a liar, adulterous, fornicator, a drunk, a drug user, or whatever before you came to God, be who you are when He chose you. You cannot be anybody but who you are. This does not mean you do drugs and still say that you are Christ-like. No, not at all. But, if you did drugs and God came into your life and changed you, go tell other drug users what God can and will do for them because He did it for you.

Whatever God made you when He found you, do not let it bother you, and do not be ashamed, just be you and God will do the rest. Do not allow your shame keep you from going back or to the church. And do not allow the shame of your past to keep you from being used by God, and doing what He has called you to do. Many times Christians in the church try to judge people by their past as if they themselves have never sinned. This should not be so. And because of these senseless acts that happens everyday the church door opens, many have fallen away from the church and have never come back. Some even died as a result of the hurt because they could not bear it. Please do not let the Blood be on your hands for judging your sister or brother and cause them to fall away from the church and from grace. God holds each one of us accountable by what we say and do [Romans 14:12]. You will give an account for pushing someone to sin and they fall away from glory/the church. Do not let it be said that it was your fault that sister Watermelon or brother Preacher never came back to your church because you yelled at her or him and talked to her or him crazy all because they were obeying what God told them to do. Do not let it be said that you pushed them away because of the secret of their past or struggle. Or, because you have taken your leadership position to the extreme as if you got it on your own and no one, not even God can tell you how to run it. No one has a stone in their hand that should be ready to throw it [John 8:7]. It will be thrown back in their face with judgment because we all have sinned and fallen short of God's glory [Romans 3:23, 1 John 1:10]. Each of us should be thankful to God for His mercy and grace that comes to give each of us another chance at getting it right when we make a mistake—we each have another opportunity to get it right and to perfect those areas in our lives that are struggles for improvement.

LET EM' TALK:

It is important to let people say what they want to say without providing strife or discord as a retaliation. Let me break it down. It is important to let people say what they want to say without you running up to them with a back hand to the mouth and face. You cannot control the way people talk or can you control what they have to say about you. My siblings and I used to chant this riddle when we were young, *"sticks and stones may break my bones but names will never hurt me."* I encourage you to hold on to this riddle. Names should never hurt you no matter who they are coming from or what names are being thrown at you. **Let em' talk.** If this is holding you back from going either back to church or to church, do not allow it to any further. Do not allow people's opinions, because that is all they are, opinions, to keep you from receiving the blessings that God has in-store for you. It is a set up by the devil to trap your mind, and to keep you in the bondage and torment of fear to be afraid of what people think in order to keep you from being who God has designed you to be. No longer will you be robbed of opportunities, blessings, change, freedom, and the peace that God so longs to give to you if you just obey Him. I challenge you to obey what I am saying to you today, go back to church and allow God to heal and to cleanse you from hurt and from what people think about you. People will never care whether God blesses you or not. They will always have something to say about everything. So this shows you that you will never win with people or with the enemy. But I want you to know that **you will win with God**. God will put loving, trust worthy people/Christians around you that are for you. They will love and help you and will encourage you and be with you. But be careful not to look at them like God. They are sent to help and to be with you, but they will never be perfect like God, nor will they take His place. You two are covenant together and should work and walk together as God leads you.

DO NOT ALLOW PEOPLE TO PUT YOU IN A BOX:

Do not allow people to put you in a box because you have not been back in the church for over a year, years, or even a decade or two. Or, maybe you have never been in a church. Your salvation is not wrapped up in theirs. What I mean by that is they do not have a Heaven or hell to put you in. So their opinions do not matter. Many times Christians are going through the same hurt or greater situation than what you are going through. They may fake and phony like nothing is wrong and their lives are perfect, but they are experiencing worse than you are. At times this may be the reason of their evil actions and persecutions towards you because they hate themselves and the positions they are facing. Do not be lured by this. It is the trick of the enemy. It is God's plan that you keep your eyes solely on Him and not on people. Where we go wrong is when we take our eyes off of God, and start focusing them on people, and then we fall. Just as Peter did as he began walking on water towards Jesus [Matthew14:22-32]. Once he took his eyes off of Jesus, he began to fall *[sink]*. This is the same for you. Keep your eyes on Christ, you cannot fail and certainly He will not fail you as you keep your eyes on Him. Amen? Do you receive that? I knew you would.

STAY IN YOUR PLACE:

1. **STORY 1-** There was a true story of a friend who shared with me concerning a pastor opening the doors of his church for another pastor and his church because something happened to his church and they no longer had it. The pastor allowed the other pastor to come on board as an associate pastor to help him out. However, as time went on, some of the congregation began to like the associate pastor better than the presiding pastor. Due to the great response, the associate pastor decided to leave and start his own church. When he left, he took almost the entire congregation with him. The presiding pastor was so hurt because he helped him and welcomed the pastor and his church in. He felt as if he had been betrayed and that the pastor schemed against him and his church, and betrayed his trust.

Pastors and leaders must be careful to stay in their places by listening to the Holy Spirit as a guide and not be led by their own bright ideas, egos, and getting caught up in the response of being a celebrity of a congregation because God uses you greatly. It is important to always remember that God is the celebrity. We as leaders and God's people are only servants who serve God and serve for God only. We are never to out shine the Lord, because we can't anyway.

What are your thoughts on this true story? Do you agree? What would you have done?

What would you do if this story were you and your life? How would you handle it better?

God did not open the door for the associate pastor to come in and steal the church's congregation. God brought him in there to help, sit under the pastor until God fully restored the associate pastor and his church the right way. The right way would not have removed members from the presiding church's pastor and brought confusion, but it would have brought order and the assignment would have been fulfilled the right way. Order would have given them a righteous farewell when it was the pastor and his church's time to leave.

A question to ask yourself, do you think the pastor was sent to the church by God? Do you believe the associate pastor betrayed the pastor of that church? Do you think the pastor was wrong in moving like he did and stealing almost the entire congregation? What would you have done if you were the presiding pastor?

2. **STORY 2-** Here is another story I have had an experience in the past while being in the clergy. There was a time a woman in ministry decided that she wanted to be a minister and decided that she was going to go through all of the proper channels to do it without praying and hearing from God first. As time went on, others around her noticed her behavior was nothing of a minister. She was out of place and certainly not in the right lane/place. She became a problem. She could not preach the gospel to everyone's understanding. She was too afraid to speak and started to talk as if she was out of place, she became withdrawn and began to cause confusion in the ministry whenever she showed up to serve, she had problems counseling people. She was a hindrance rather than a help. God will never call a person to a particular ministry that they are not ready for, nor will He call a person in the ministry that will cause confusion and He cannot get the glory. God will also never call a person in the ministry that they cannot operate in it effectively. It is only to do His Will effectively in order that He will use that person in a way that that person will be in their proper place so that lives will change and not become worse. In this story, her attitude and her spirit made things worse. There were complaints all the time.

What are your thoughts on this true story? Do you agree? What do you think she should have done? _____

_____

_____

_____

_____

What would you do if this story were you and your life? How would you handle it better?

3. <u>**STORY 3-**</u> There was a married couple who already had problems in their marriage and went to a local church for help. After they joined the church and got involved in the marriage/couples ministry, the head ministry leader began to like the married couple's wife as she counseled with him about personal things in their marriage. They became close and began to mess around with each other; and made what God was trying to mend back together with the couple, only to open the door for the devil to tear apart. The couple got a divorce and their marriage was never restored. The head ministry leader and the married woman got together but they did not last six months due to the pressure and persecution they suffered within the church after they all found out.

If the people of God would just stay in their lane/place, God can do what He wants and need to do for all of His people. But when we get in the way, or get in the wrong position, or try to compete with others and get in a position God has not called, or spread lies about good people, or allow our flesh and emotions to make us fall and do things we never thought we'd do, this cancels the assignment God originally planned for us in the first place.

What are your thoughts on this true story? Do you agree? What do you think should have happened?

What would you do if this story were you and your life? How would you handle it better?

4. <u>STORY 4-</u> There was a man who struggled with the same sex who came to the church and wanted to get involved in ministry. The pastor allowed him to join the church but he, the deacon board, and some of the congregation did not let him get involve because of his struggle. He only came to the church because he liked the church and only wanted to be used by God and to get involved. When the church found out, they all laughed and made mockery of the man's struggle. The pastor made gay jokes over the pull-pit as he preached, some of the church folks snickered when the man came in the sanctuary, especially when the Holy Spirit began to touch him as his mannerisms came across in a feminine way, and they all began to laugh. The deacon board still did not approve of him getting involved. The man was so injured and hurt because he tried to make a decision to live right although he struggled. He rededicated his life back to God but

because of what it looked like on the outside, the deacon board and the church folks assumed he was not delivered and made false accusations and decisions.

As a result, it cost them to lose a great man of God who could have been used by God in a mighty way and the opportunity to save others. The man soon left the church through church hurt, gave up, and went back out there and got back in the same sin he had been delivered from. The church erred because they did not seek God nor did they pray and know what the Word of God says about no one having the right to judge but God. No one can say that a person is not free but God. It is only between God and that man concerning the struggle he had. No one has a right to throw stones because the same stone you throw are the same stones coming back to you from your hand or worse. The Word of God says, "He who is without sin, let him cast the first stone" [John 8:3-11].

The fact that the church were not set free or struggled with the same sin as the man did, caused them to have a prideful, judgmental, insensitive spirit that pushed someone who could have been a powerful enforcement to the Body of Christ. Just because their struggle possibly was not the same as what the man had, did not mean that they were any better, nor did it mean that they were without sin. In fact, they could possibly have had the same struggle but tried to hide it. Or, they could have had a struggle that was worse.

If the church judged you in the same way—to magnify your struggle/sin to the entire church, how would you feel? God has not called any of us to attack or to act as if we never sinned or as if we make decisions in the church. God is the only One Who should make decisions as His people seek Him first for an answer.

God can use anybody the way He so chooses. The Word of God says, "We all have sinned and fallen short of God's glory" [Romans 3:23]. No one is exempt.

When we as the people of God learn to pray, be led by the Holy Spirit, <u>love all people</u>, and stay in our places, we will be much more further in getting to the place where God what's us to be. It is a challenge being in ministry but this is why it is important to allow God to be your guide and allow only Him to lead you, your love walk, your decision making, and to constantly be reminded the fact that you are no more better than the sinner, you've just been saved by grace.

What are your thoughts on this story? Do you agree? What do you think should have been done better? If you were in the church would you have judged the man in the same way?

What would you do if this story were you and your life? How would you handle it better?

Conclusion

◊   ◊   ◊   ◊   ◊   ◊   ◊

HANK YOU FOR GIVING MY BOOK A TRY. It must have caught your eye in some sort of way, or someone told you about it, or just maybe you are going through this right now and could identify with the title of the book that made you want to pick it up and read it. Are you glad you did? I sure hope so. There are millions of Christians that can identify with this book. Millions are hurting as a result of church hurt. This book, "Church Hurt" is from a realist point of view. All of my books are from a realist point of view. So I encourage you to read all of my other books as well. I guarantee you that they each will minister to you in some sort of way.

> *There are millions of Christians that can identify with this book. And millions are hurting as a result of church hurt.*
>
> *"Church Hurt" is from a realist point of view.*

We as the people of God and as the body of Christ that makes up the church are on a mandate to grab a hold of the heart of God. We are to grab a hold of His plan and purpose for His church, and to bring His Holy Spirit back in the hurting church. He is full of mercy. He is full of grace. He wants to give the church the victory. He is full glory and majesty. He strives for us to glorify Him with our praise and worship. He strives for us to edify Him with our gifts through the five-fold ministry

(Apostle, Prophet, Evangelist, Preacher, and Teacher), for the perfecting of the saints, to edify, equip and involve every child of God who is saved through Jesus Christ; and to build a whole, carefree, faith, bible based church in these last and evil days. It is the Will of God that the saints of God come in the unity of the faith; strive to obtain the heart of Jesus and all knowledge of His Word, and press daily to be as perfect as possible through the stature and fullness of His Name.

The Life Changer Experience

◊   ◊   ◊   ◊   ◊   ◊   ◊

9   **HAVE TO ASK. ARE YOU RIGHT** with the Lord? If not, I do not want to wait to give you a chance to change your life to a better, wholesome, freedom filled lifestyle.

If you know your life is not what it needs to be and you're ready to get it together, repeat the lines below:

Lord I know you are real. My life is not what it needs to be and I'm ready to change it. You said in Romans 10:9 that if I CONFESS with my mouth and BELIEVE in my heart that You were raised from the dead, I shall be saved and my life will never be the same. So I CONFESS that you are Lord, Savior and Redeemer and you died just for my sins. Take control of everything and everybody that is in my life. Use me for your purpose and glory in Jesus Name, Amen.

By repeating, confessing, and believing the paragraph above, you have just become a child of God and your life will never be the same. May God bless you as you find a church home if you do not already have one, and get active in the church and allow God to use your spiritual gifts for His glory.

QUESTIONS ON A PERSONAL LEVEL:

1. After reading this book, how will you choose to forgive those in the church who has hurt you? _____

    _____

    _____

    _____

2. _____ has hurt me and I am choosing to release them today. I am going to do it by _____

    _____

    _____

    _____

3. I have experienced church hurt by _____

    _____

    _____

    _____

4. Scriptures I am going to stand on _____

    _____

    _____

Use additional space below for personal level documentation.

NOTE PAD FOR NOTE TAKING

After reading this book my life has changed...

ADDITIONAL SCRIPTURES FOR HEALING

Rejection & Depression:

Isaiah 61:3

Heaviness:

Isaiah 61:3, John 15:26, Matthew 18:18

Inner Hurts:

Luke 4:18, Proverbs 18:14; 26:22

Suicidal Thoughts:

Mark 9

Self-Pity:

Psalm 69:20

Sorrow-Grief:

Nehemiah 2:2, Proverbs 15:13

Insomnia *(Inability to Sleep)*:

Nehemiah 2:2

How to Get Free from Strongholds of Hurt, Fear, and Anger:

2 Corinthians 10:4-5, I John 4:18

Broken-Heart:

Psalm 69:20, Proverbs 12:18; 15:3, 13; 18:14, Luke 4:18

Deliverance From the Battle in Your Mind:

Romans 12:2, Jeremiah 4:14

Personal Prayer of Deliverance & Healing:

Father, I come to You thanking You for being my Healer and My deliverer. Without you, there is no other. I thank You that I am healed from all that oppress me. I will choose this day to no longer be a slave for the devil to torment me and make me a prisoner to his evil tactics to keep me bound. I thank You that I am healed from hurt, anger, depression, oppression, fear, and hatred. They no longer belong to me. In Jesus Name, Amen.

BOOKS BY STEPHANIE

FICTION NOVELS & MOTIVATIONAL BOOKS:

1. When Ramona Got Her Groove Back from God
2. My Song of Solomon
3. My Song of Solomon *Prayer Journal*
4. God Loves Thugs Too!
5. The Locker Room Experience: *For the Struggling Athlete & Coach, & Tips on How to Get Recruited in Sports*

MINISTRY BOOKS & WORKBOOK:

6. Position Your Faith for Great Success
7. Position Your Faith for Great Success *Workbook*
8. The Purpose Chaser: *For Children Ages 5 to 12*
9. Church Hurt: *How to Heal & Overcome It*

To Reorder Books or request book signings, speaking engagements, and/or workshops and/or seminars, email or visit Website(s):

Stephanie Franklin Ministries
info@stephaniefranklinministries.org
www.stephaniefranklinministries.org
www.heavenlyrealmpublishing.com
1-866-216-0696, EXT. 1

Stephanie Franklin Ministries
PO Box 682532
Houston, TX 77268

Join Today!

Become A Purpose Chaser!

When you join the Purpose Chasers through Stephanie Franklin Ministries, you are saying that "I'm going to chase after my purpose and dreams no matter what. I am going to chase after God with all I have no matter what nobody says. I'm going to chase with a good attitude, I am going to chase in my home, in my community, in my school, in my church; all over the world."

JOIN TODAY! VISIT:
www.stephaniefranklinministries.org

YOU MAY ALSO EMAIL ME TODAY!
info@stephaniefranklinministries.org

Order Your, "I'm A Purpose Chaser" T-Shirt today!

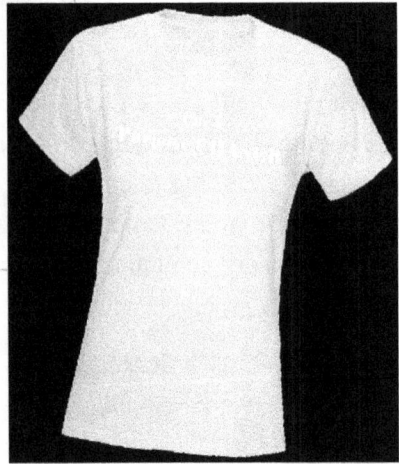

VISIT MY WEBSITE TO ORDER:

www.stephaniefranklinministries.org

Or send email for accurate size and price:

info@stephaniefranklinministries.org

Stephanie Franklin, M.A. (T. S.)

is the author of, When Ramona Got Her Groove Back from God, My Song of Solomon, My Song of Solomon *Prayer Journal*, Position Your Faith for Great Success, Position Your Faith for Great Success *Workbook*, The Purpose Chaser: *For Children Ages 5 to 12*, God Loves Thugs Too!, and now her **two new releases**: Church Hurt: *How to Heal & Overcome It and*

The Locker Room Experience: *For the Struggling Athlete & Coach, & Tips on How to Get Recruited in Sports.*

Stephanie has a vision to reach the world with her mentoring, teaching, life coaching and preaching ministry. She has a heart to reach the youth and young adults along with the entire family, bringing them all together as a unified fold.

She has received her Master of Arts Degree in Theological Studies. Her mission while on this earth is to be used by God in whatever capacity He chooses.

She enjoys spending time with family and friends.

www.ingramcontent.com/pod-product-compliance
Lightning Source LLC
Chambersburg PA
CBHW071836090426
42737CB00012B/2257